Customers & Consumerism

ISSUES

Volume 134

Series Editor

Lisa Firth

Independence

Educational Publishers

Cambridge

First published by Independence
PO Box 295
Cambridge CB1 3XP
England

British Library Cataloguing in Publication Data
Customers and Consumerism – (Issues Series)
I. Firth, Lisa II. Series
381.3'0941

ISBN 978 1 86168 386 1

Printed in Great Britain
MWL Print Group Ltd

Cover
The illustration on the front cover is by
Angelo Madrid.

CONTENTS

Chapter One: Consumer Trends

Chapter Two: Rights and Risks

Chapter Three: Ethical Consumerism

Introduction

Customers and Consumerism is the one hundred and thirty-fourth volume in the *Issues* series. The aim of this series is to offer up-to-date information about important issues in our world.

Customers and Consumerism looks at consumer trends, the risks associated with being a consumer, consumer rights and being an ethical consumer.

The information comes from a wide variety of sources and includes:
Government reports and statistics
Newspaper reports and features
Magazine articles and surveys
Website material
Literature from lobby groups
and charitable organisations.

It is hoped that, as you read about the many aspects of the issues explored in this book, you will critically evaluate the information presented. It is important that you decide whether you are being presented with facts or opinions. Does the writer give a biased or an unbiased report? If an opinion is being expressed, do you agree with the writer?

Customers and Consumerism offers a useful starting-point for those who need convenient access to information about the many issues involved. However, it is only a starting-point. Following each article is a URL to the relevant organisation's website, which you may wish to visit for further information.

* * * * *

Consumers

Information from Consumer Education

Who is a consumer?

We all are because we are all users. We use goods and services every day. We need food, warmth and shelter. We travel on buses or trains, visit the doctor or dentist, go to the library, have a haircut, go to the cinema or watch television. At home we use energy in the form of gas, electricity, coal or oil. We expect clean, drinkable water from the tap. If we put out the dustbin we expect the local council's refuse collection service to pick it up and empty it. We demand a minimum standard of education and health care and we rely on the police to help safeguard our property.

We are all consumers because we are all users. We use goods and services every day

Consumer rights and responsibilities

Being a good consumer means knowing what to look out for and what to avoid. It means knowing where and how to get the best value for money, where to go if things go wrong. Your role as a consumer has both rights and responsibilities; for example:

The right to choose

Consumer choice is something you might take for granted because you expect to be able to walk into a shop and take your pick from a selection of brands. Suppliers compete with one another to attract attention and tempt you to buy their products and shop in their stores as opposed to those of their rivals. You might use a shop because it's near your home, because the prices are reasonable or because it always has what you want.

You may be mad about beef-burgers and choose one brand because you think they taste best and have more meat and less fat than the others. Or you may use a particular shampoo because you believe it makes your hair look shiny and feel soft.

Supposing that you weren't given the option because there was only one company making beef-burgers and one making shampoo, and there was only one place that sold them? You'd have to take whatever they offered and pay whatever they asked or go without. You'd have no real choice. Competition between suppliers means that customers get a better deal because it keeps traders on their toes. They have to change and respond to consumer demand or risk going out of business. Consumer choice can be an effective means of influencing production because by refusing to accept shoddy or over-priced goods and services you can force suppliers to change their ideas. You as a consumer can encourage competition and help improve quality – if you use your right to choose.

The right to accurate information

Suppliers of goods and services should give out clear and accurate information so that you, the consumer, are able to make meaningful comparisons and can choose what is best suited to your individual needs.

Sometimes the law demands that information is provided e.g. the law says that beef-burgers have to be labelled with a list of ingredients including additives like artificial colourings or preservatives. You could be allergic to some chemicals and need to know what to look out for and what to avoid. If you buy a shirt or blouse then the law says that the label must tell you what fabric it is made from. This could be important if you have sensitive skin and need to avoid certain fibres.

Sometimes suppliers are allowed to choose what information or detail they provide. It's up to you to find out what you think you need to know and to use that information to help you make your choice. If you think that you've been deliberately cheated or conned by misleading information

then the law is on your side. It's up to you to make a complaint about it.

The right to safety

You have the right to be sure that products are not going to put your life or health in danger. The law on safety is very strict and demands that suppliers meet certain basic minimum standards. Often manufacturers will have to carry out rigorous safety tests and checks before they are allowed to put goods into the shops. Motorcycle crash helmets, for instance, have to pass a series of high impact tests and be marked with the British Standards Institution's Kite mark. Other goods must be labelled with warnings or clear instructions for use. It's your responsibility to read and follow the instructions carefully and you can't blame the manufacturer or supplier if you choose to ignore the warnings. If you are unlucky enough to be injured because the product was dangerous or the warning unclear then you ought to report it – if only to save someone else from getting hurt. Trading Standards Department can help.

The right to value for money

No one enjoys feeling that they've been cheated or conned into paying a high price for poor quality. But it can happen, unless you look carefully at what you're buying.

Remember that 'value' doesn't always mean 'cheapest'. Instead it means that the standard or quality ought to be reflected in the price. Whether you think that something is worth its asking price is for you to decide. If you buy a pair of expensive jeans and pay far more than the average price for them, you might expect them to last, to keep their shape and to wear well. If you buy a much cheaper pair you may not worry if they go baggy in places and wear thin at the knees after a much shorter time. You often have to strike a reasonable balance between cost and quality. It can be unreasonable to expect the highest standard at the lowest price. You've probably heard the expression 'You only get what you pay for'.

No one enjoys feeling that they've been cheated or conned into paying a high price for poor quality. But it can happen, unless you look carefully at what you're buying

---

Of course you may be lucky and pick up a genuine bargain in the sales. You should still make sure that the reduced price isn't simply to make up for a reduction in quality, and that you're buying something you really want. It's no saving at all if you're left with something you can't use.

The right to redress

This has nothing to do with putting on your clothes again. It means that as a consumer you have the right to complain and to have your complaint settled fairly. No matter how careful you may have been there's still a chance that something may go wrong. If it does then you may ask for some sort of compensation. Most shops or suppliers would be willing to help because they believe that a satisfied customer is one who will come back again and spend more money. The law helps, too, because it lays down the rules for fair and honest trading. It says, that if you buy faulty goods then you can return them immediately and ask for a refund, or if you book a holiday and the travel agent switches your destination at the last minute, you're entitled to compensation.

You've got to do something too. It's up to you to find out about your legal rights. No one else is going to do it for you. If you aren't certain about what you're entitled to and how to go about getting it, then get some advice.

⇨ The above information is reprinted with kind permission from Consumer Education. Visit www.consumereducation.org.uk for more information.

© *Consumer Education*

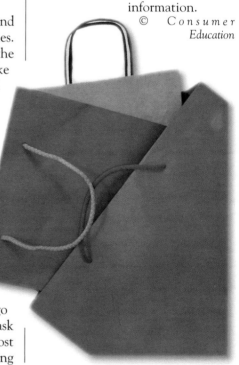

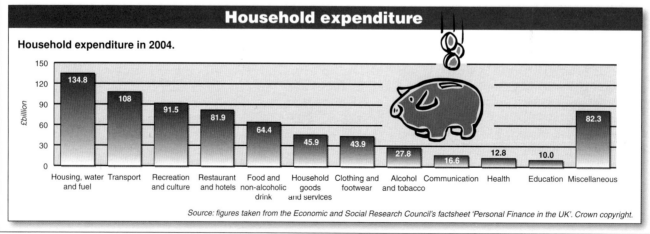

Household expenditure

Household expenditure in 2004.

Category	£billion
Housing, water and fuel	134.8
Transport	108
Recreation and culture	91.5
Restaurant and hotels	81.9
Food and non-alcoholic drink	64.4
Household goods and services	45.9
Clothing and footwear	43.9
Alcohol and tobacco	27.8
Communication	16.6
Health	12.8
Education	10.0
Miscellaneous	82.3

Source: figures taken from the Economic and Social Research Council's factsheet 'Personal Finance in the UK'. Crown copyright.

Consumer spending

British spending hits a record high of £1 trillion

Latest research from Mintel's flagship British Lifestyles report finds that spending has hit a record high as British consumers parted with as much as £1 trillion (a million million) last year alone. On average this works out at around £37,000 for every household across Britain today. These levels of spending* show a massive 43% increase in real terms (once inflation has been taken into account) on 1995 figures, when spend stood at just a little over £540 billion.

In real terms, growth over the last decade has been greatest in the 'considered expenditure' arena, which includes all big ticket purchases such as holidays, cars, furniture and appliances. Collectively these markets experienced an impressive 57% growth over the ten years to 2005. This is compared to 51% growth in 'housing and finance' and a 49% increase in 'occasional expenditure', which are basic necessities, that need some consideration before purchasing, such as clothing, kitchenware and going out. The smallest growth was seen in 'everyday expenditure', including food and drink, tobacco, printed media, medication and toiletries, which grew by only 18% over the same ten-year period.

'The £1 trillion mark is a significant milestone in the expansion of the British consumer economy. The last ten years have clearly been the decade of big ticket purchases and the buoyant expenditure on these items such as holidays, cars, furniture and appliances reflects the growing affluence of the British nation as a whole,' comments Paul Rickard, Director of Research at Mintel.

Holidays: Wish you were here...?

Today, holidays are the number one luxury or non-essential area of spending, exceeded only by house purchases and alterations, life assurance, food and the combined

MINTeL

cost of rent, council tax and water. Together holidays and travel insurance now account for around a third of 'considered expenditure', with spend increasing some 19% between 1995 and 2005 to reach almost £47.5 billion or some £790 a year for every man, woman and child in Britain today.

Spending has hit a record high as British consumers parted with as much as £1 trillion (a million million) in 2005 alone

---

'Despite a series of devastating natural disasters and terrorism attacks in key holiday destinations since the start of the millennium, the British have proved to be a resilient lot and are now travelling abroad more than ever before. Enthusiasm whetted over the years by the availability of cheap package deals and cheap air travel is undoubtedly fuelling a taste for more unusual adventurous holidays, sometimes in more exotic destinations. It is also now not uncommon for families to go on several vacations a year with the trend very much moving towards shorter but more frequent breaks,' comments Paul Rickard.

Home appliances: Switch on to new technology

Looking at other big ticket purchases, domestic appliances, including white and brown goods, home computers and laundry appliances such as washing machines and dryers, have

seen a significant level of growth over the past decade. The market as a whole increased 58% in real terms to be worth £12.3 billion, representing around £475 spend per household a year or the equivalent of a good quality washing machine each year.

At the start of the decade white goods dominated the domestic appliances market, accounting for almost half the value, with brown goods, laundry appliances and small/home computers languishing some way behind. But today brown goods, such as TVs and DVD players, are the largest sector (47%), with the switch happening at the start of the millennium.

The brown goods sector and home computers are the two areas that have seen the greatest levels of growth over the past decade. Brown goods have experienced growth of some 642% in real terms, generating total sales of £5.8 billion, while home computers have seen 695% growth, demonstrating the rise of working from home. However, both these sectors have experienced considerable price deflation. The price of these products usually falls rapidly after they are first put on the market and growth in these sectors was 108% and 123% respectively over the ten-year period once this had been taken into account.

'Despite the maturity of the brown goods market, sales of products such as TVs and stereos have not suffered since reaching the point where almost every household has one, they have in fact thrived. The televisions market in particular has been fast moving and driven by developments such as the emergence of widescreen formats, flatscreen technologies, digital sound and vision, and advances in broadcasting capacities. The introduction of DVD players has also given this sector a real boost but this has undoubtedly been at the expense of spend on video players,' explains Paul Rickard.

'The British are far more likely to upgrade a TV, stereo or even home computer before it has reached the end of its life, a trend that is not as apparent in the market for the more mundane appliances, such as washing machines, tumble dryers or dishwashers.'

Furniture and furnishings: Britain sees the light

The total market for furniture and furnishings has grown strongly (21%) since 1995, to reach £13.8 billion last year, equating to £534 per household per year. Domestic lighting, the smallest sector within the furniture and furnishings market, has shown the fastest growth, up some 60% to £809 million in 2005.

'Lighting has been propelled by consumers' increasing sophistication and understanding of how room lighting can be used as a quick and easy makeover. In addition, there has been faster growth in more expensive options such as halogen lamps, the energy-efficient CFLs and spotlights,' explains Paul Rickard.

The floorcoverings sector (worth some £1.9 billion) has shown the slowest growth by value at just 8% since 2005, with this sector characterised by intense price competition from cheaper imports of carpets, rugs and smooth coverings, such as vinyl and wood laminate. Despite this, smooth floorcoverings are now regularly used to make a smaller room appear more spacious, which will remain an issue in today's often compact homes and demand has shown real increases, with consumers also appreciating its clean modern look as an alternative to carpet.

Motoring: Used-car salesmen drive Britain's car market

Total expenditure on motoring (including car purchase, servicing and security, motorcycles and mopeds) exceeded £65.5 billion in 2005, with the market growing 35% in real terms between 1995 and 2005. When it comes to car sales alone, new models provide all the buzz and excitement in the market, but they (whether of new or existing models) only accounted for 29% of total car sales last year. It is in fact used cars that now make up the largest sector, taking 59% of the market, with the remaining 12% accounted for by company cars used for private motoring. While the new cars sector lost value over the decade, used cars increased sales by 152% to be worth £23.2 billion. This is double the new car market, a particularly impressive achievement as spend on used cars only overtook new car sales in 1998.

'The used car sector is the real bread and butter of the market and it has been consistently increasing its sales and total share year on year,' comments Paul Rickard.

Housing: Home is where the heart (and money) is

Beyond 'considered expenditure' Britain spent an impressive £327.5 billion on the place we call home last year alone, making housing the biggest area of spending. In 2005, the British lavished an additional 69% in real terms on housing – which includes anything from house purchase, rent and council tax to home repairs, maintenance and insurance – compared to 1995. Although spending in 2005 saw an increase of 4.2% or some £13 billion on 2004 figures, this actually represents a significant slowdown after successive years of rapid growth (21.2% in 2002, 17.9% in 2003 and 9.7% in 2004). The number of housing transactions fell by almost 25% between 2004 and 2005 to reach 1.23 million – the lowest total since 1995 (1.19 million).

'Last year saw the housing market stagnate as some buyers, particularly first-time buyers, decided to wait and see how prices would move before they committed to buying a house. The slowdown in the property market with stagnant house prices, less borrowing on home loans and fewer approvals for house purchases all contributed to the lower growth in overall spending on housing during 2005,' explains Paul Rickard.

Finance: Britain's borrowing grinding to a halt?

Total expenditure on insurance and pension products increased by 36% over the ten years to 2005 to reach £123 billion, some way behind the peak of £142 billion of 2000. That said, consumer expenditure on both personal and occupational pensions has recently started to edge up as people realise that they must bolster their retirement provision. With reliance on state pensions not an option for many, spending on pensions looks set to increase over the next decade.

When it comes to borrowing, net consumer credit peaked at £23 billion in 2004 as the 'credit boom' saw ever-increasing levels of borrowing, particularly on credit cards and personal loans. But between 2004 and 2005 the amount consumers borrowed over and above what they paid back fell by a massive 28% to just under £17 billion as consumers clearly started to become more sensible about their borrowing habits.

* all spend on goods and services, as well as contributions to pensions and other financial products, council tax and an assessment of true housing costs.

About Mintel

Mintel is a worldwide leader of competitive media, product and consumer intelligence. For more than 35 years, Mintel has provided key insight into leading global trends. With offices in Chicago, London, Belfast and Sydney, Mintel's innovative product line provides unique data that has a direct impact on client success. For more information on Mintel, please visit their website at www.mintel.com. *March 2006*

⇨ The above information is reprinted with kind permission from Mintel. Visit www.mintel.com for more information.

© *Mintel*

Consumer durables

79% of households have a mobile phone

The ownership of consumer durables in the UK continued to increase into 2005-06.

The proportion of households owning a home computer rose from 62 per cent to 65 per cent between 2004-05 and 2005-06 and from 33 per cent in 1998-99. The percentage of households with an internet connection also rose, from 10 per cent in 1998-99 to 55 per cent in 2005-06.

In the highest income group, 95 per cent of households owned a home computer and 93 per cent had an internet connection. This compares to 29 per cent of households in the lowest income group who owned a home computer and 17 per cent who had an internet connection.

The proportion of households owning a home computer rose from 62 per cent to 65 per cent between 2004-05 and 2005-06 and from 33 per cent in 1998-99

The percentage of households with access to a dishwasher and microwave continued to rise, to 35 per cent and 91 per cent respectively in 2005-06. Ownership of a CD player increased from 68 per cent in 1998-99 to 88 per cent in 2005-06.

There was also a considerable increase in the proportion of households with a mobile phone since 1998-99 (from 27 per cent to 79 per cent). In 2005-06, 56 per cent of households in the lowest income group reported owning a mobile phone, compared to 45 per cent in 2004-05.

In 2005-06 most homes had central heating (94 per cent), a washing machine (95 per cent) and a telephone (92 per cent).

Source
Expenditure and Food Survey, Office for National Statistics

Notes
The consumer durables covered by the Expenditure and Food Survey are:

Central heating, Washing machine, Tumble dryer, Dishwasher, Microwave, Telephone, Mobile phone, Video recorder, Satellite receiver, CD player, Home computer, Internet connection.

Published on 18 January 2007

The ownership of consumer durables such as mobile phones and MP3 players continued to increase into 2005-06

⇨ The above information is reprinted with kind permission from the Office for National Statistics. Visit www.statistics.gov.uk for more information.

© Crown copyright

Affluenza

The new middle-class 'mental illness'

'Mindless consumerism' is fuelling emotional health problems, clinical psychologist Oliver James claims.

In his new book *Affluenza*, the television psychologist argues that the middle-class pursuit of material 'success' is fuelling problems like depression and anxiety.

James toured seven nations interviewing 240 people from Cornwall to Cambridge and Singapore to Sydney, before concluding that 'selfish capitalism' has run riot.

He found that the middle class rigorously pursue consumer goals, such as a larger house, promotion or new car.

But James told Reuters: 'Studies in lots of different nations show that if you place high value on those things, you are more likely to suffer depression, anxiety, addictions and personality disorders.'

Affluenza warns that people in English-speaking nations are now twice as likely to suffer from poor emotional health as those in mainland western European nations.

However, James is hopeful that the mood is right for change, pointing out that his analysis dovetails with the environmental conclusion that the present level of consumerism is not sustainable.

26 January 2007

⇨ The above information is reprinted with kind permission from Adfero. Visit www.adfero.co.uk for more information.

© Adfero

Companies branded 'out of touch' by consumers

Many companies are in the dark about what annoys consumers and forces them to take their business elsewhere, reveals a new National Consumer Council survey into customer service

Half of consumers said that, when faced with problems in the last year, they didn't complain because procedures are too long-winded and tiresome.

Being kept on hold for ages or passed endlessly around voice-activated phone systems were listed as consumers' biggest gripes in this latest research in association with Andrew Smith Research. Irritation with incompetent call centre staff and condescending attitudes followed close behind.

NCC Deputy Chief Executive Philip Cullum says:

'Over 80% of consumers tell us they would be only too pleased to help companies get better, but many businesses still seem distant and unaware of customers' real experiences. Half of those who had been let down or treated badly said it was just easier to go somewhere else than sort out their present difficulties.

'With 70% of consumers believing company bosses are out of touch, with no idea what it's like to be a customer, it's time for businesses to get smart and put their customers at the heart.'

The findings echo NCC's recent *Stupid Company* report that uncovered a growing consumer backlash against shoddy service across a range of sectors.

When asked to pick out the company where they've experienced the best customer service, Tesco came out top, followed by Asda, BT and First Direct, with Nationwide and the Virgin Group joint fifth. Top of the list of worst offenders were local councils, followed by NTL, BT (again), British Gas and the Royal Mail.

Notes

1. NCC's survey of consumer satisfaction was conducted in association with Andrew Smith Research. A nationally representative sample of 1051 adults, aged 18+, responded online from 2-7 March 2006. Respondents were members of the Research Now! online panel of consumers.
2. Andrew Smith Research is a leading independent consultancy specialising in research for leisure, travel, media and other service sector clients.
3. Research Now! is a leading provider of online research, and operates the Valued Opinions pan-el of 250,000 UK households. For more information please visit their website.
4. *The Stupid Company* (6 February 2006) sets out the results of an extensive programme of NCC research, conducted over almost 18 months. The report is available on the website.

12 April 2006

➪ The above information is reprinted with kind permission from the National Consumer Council. For more information on this and other topics, please visit the National Consumer Council website at www.ncc.org.uk

© *National Consumer Council*

Key findings

a) Top customer service problems consumers experience:
➪ Being left on hold for long periods
➪ Telephone voice-activated phone systems
➪ Telephone staff who are not competent to help
➪ Arrogant or condescending attitudes from call centre staff

b) I've wanted to complain about a company over the last year, but it was such an effort I didn't bother.
Agree 49%, Disagree 29%, Don't know 22%

c) When a company lets me down or annoys me, I don't usually tell them – I just take my business elsewhere
Agree 50%, Disagree 35%, Don't know 15%

d) The people running big companies really do understand what it feels like to be a consumer
Agree 10%, Disagree 70%, Don't know 20%

e) I am happy to give companies feedback if I know they'll act on it
Agree 84%, Disagree 3%, Don't know 13%

Best provider of customer service over the past year:
➪ Tesco
➪ Asda
➪ BT
➪ First Direct
➪ Nationwide & Virgin group

Worst provider of customer service over the past year:
➪ Local council
➪ NTL
➪ BT
➪ British Gas
➪ Post Office/Royal Mail

Advertising

What is advertising?

Advertising today is a major industry. Each year between 1-2% of all income in the UK is spent on advertising. Without advertising, there would be no radio or television, very few magazines and newspapers and no 'free' newspapers.

Most advertising is communication between sellers and potential buyers [consumers and other producers]. Advertisements should be informative but some advertisements contain no words, only colours and pictures and the brand name.

Demand can be affected by advertising. But, producers could also introduce 'new' products to increase sales or pack the product differently. An individual's wants are determined by age, tastes and status.

Advertising today is a major industry. Each year between 1-2% of all income in the UK is spent on advertising

---

The Trade Description Act has been broken if an advertisement contains an error. Misleading adverts should be reported to:
⇨ Trading Standards
⇨ Advertising Standards Authority

A newspaper never knowingly publishes a misleading advertisement as 'conditions' clearly state that advertisers must not breach the law. The Advertising Standards Authority is funded by the newspaper industry to make sure that the worst examples of misleading advertisements never appear. There is always the unscrupulous seller who will try to deceive both the newspaper and the buyer e.g. the trader who tries to pretend he is just a private individual selling his own goods. You have far fewer rights when buying from non-

The case of the falling flake: the problem

Cadbury's Flake had been a top-selling chocolate bar with sales growing steadily until 1977 when the whole confectionery market went into decline. Sales dropped by 7%, but Flake lost 13% of its sales. They had to find the reason for the fall and try to reverse the trend.

Research: They had to find out as much as possible about the product, who bought it and why people liked or disliked it. People who were most likely to buy Flake were women aged 25-44 who saw the bar as an 'individual, self-indulgent treat'. Men and women of all ages bought the bar occasionally, but were put off by the 'messiness' of eating it. The agency decided to concentrate on this group and develop a new campaign.

The Strategy: People ate the 'crumbs' in different ways so they decided to turn the 'messiness' disadvantage into an advantage by making it a positive selling feature. The new campaign showed people eating the last crumbs in their own individual way. A bowler-hat commuter on a train tipped crumbs onto a paper plate and used it as a funnel; a freckled-faced schoolboy sucked them through a straw; and someone tipped back a swivel chair to eat them. The slogan was 'Every piece of Flake is sheer enjoyment, so take care not to miss a morsel'.

Testing and Results: To see if the new advert worked, it was screened in two TV areas only and sales were watched. After 18 months, the new campaign had increased sales by 16% in the test areas and more men bought the product. When the campaign was extended to London, sales increased by 230%, but their original buyers – women aged 25-44 – were buying less because they didn't like the new advert. The agency decided to run both campaigns together proving it was possible to attract new buyers by giving the product a fresher image yet keeping their traditional buyers happy.

traders. If a car you bought turned out to be a bike, you could only sue for a false description. If the seller was a trader, the car would have to be of a reasonable standard, and terms like 'sold as seen' would be illegal. If the car didn't meet its description or was un-roadworthy the Trading Standards Department could prosecute.

Advertising is:
⇨ Big Business with a turnover of over £3,579 million in Britain.
⇨ More than just a TV or radio commercial. 22% of advertising money is spent on classified ads – the sort used by anyone to sell anything from old television sets and cars to cookers and pets. Posters, sponsorship, design of carrier bags, car stickers and badges, are all forms of advertising.

⇨ Expensive. A 30-second commercial shown at peak time will cost hundreds of thousands of pounds to produce and screen. An advertiser will employ a professional agency to put a campaign together to produce the finished product.
⇨ Effective. Manufacturers think so or why would they spend so much money on it? Expensive advertising campaigns encourage shopkeepers and customers.
⇨ A social phenomenon. Advertising is all around us and is often striking, thought provoking or amusing, and many slogans and catchphrases find their way into everyday language. Advertising creates social trends and feminist groups criticise advertising for portraying women either as sex objects or as domesticated

creatures whose main concern is for the whiteness of their washing. Groups concerned with poverty have criticised advertising for showing people in middle-class surroundings implying that this is how most people live. They argue that it can make poor people want to spend money on goods they don't need and that very few black people are portrayed in TV commercials yet almost 1 person in 10 in Britain is black.

When you listen to, watch, or read an advert the important thing is the message you take away with you, not what the advert actually says

---

⇨ Manipulative. To be effective, advertising has to affect the way we think and behave. We have advice from friendly window cleaners, housewives, or warm, professional dentists and doctors beaming out at us from TV screens and posters. Advertisers have to make sure that the information and advice they give us is not harmful or immoral, yet the commercial interest always comes first. In third-world countries, some advertisers have been criticised for encouraging people to spend money on sugary soft drinks rather than nourishing food.

How advertising works

If a person wants to sell his car or advertise a room in his house to let, he will usually place his own advertisement. This is likely to be in the 'classified' section of his local newspaper or by putting a card in the window of a local shop.

A major manufacturer with hundreds of thousands of pounds to spend will employ an advertising agency. The agency will act as a link between the manufacturer and creative and research people needed to put an effective campaign together. The agency will decide with the manufacturer:

⇨ what message has to be put across?
⇨ how to express the message – in words and pictures
⇨ where to say it – on radio, TV or in newspapers, magazines, on poster sites or on a combination of these.

Where to say it and who to say it to

Almost as important as planning what to say in a campaign is deciding how to get the message across. If a lot of selling points have to be put over, then magazines or newspapers are ideal because the reader has time to study the message. Most TV commercials last for only thirty seconds and so can't give out much information. With newspapers and magazines, getting the message across means talking to the right people – the people who are most likely to buy the product. This means researching who these people are and what sort of magazine they read or programmes they watch. Advertisers tend to group people together by age and by social class. Social class or grade is meant to indicate a person's spending power.

A Higher managerial, administrative and professional 2.4%
B Intermediate managerial, administrative and professional 13.5%
C1 Supervisory / clerical and junior managerial, administrative and professional 25.4%
C2 Skilled manual 24.8%
D Semi-skilled and unskilled manual 19.8%

E Casual labourers, state pensioners and the unemployed 14.1%
(Source: Advertising Association)

The cost of putting an advert in a newspaper or magazine depends on two things: the circulation (how many people read the publication) and their spending power (as measured by their social grading). Different people are likely to buy the Sun and the Guardian. Advertisers assume that the average Sun reader has less money to spend than the average Guardian reader, but a lot more people (around four million) read the Sun. So although a full-page advert in the Sun costs far more than one in the Guardian, it actually costs far less to reach each individual Sun reader. In fact, it's six times cheaper for an advertiser to talk to a Sun reader than a Guardian reader!

Images in advertising

When you listen to, watch, or read an advert the important thing is the message you take away with you, not what the advert actually says.

⇨ An advert for Hovis bread showed a delivery boy riding his bicycle through cobbled streets with the voice of an old man recalling his youth to the sound of a brass band in the background. The setting and background music gave the idea that the product was old-fashioned, wholesome and delicious, although no one actually said so.
⇨ Animated cartoons of countryside full of birds, butterflies and

cows are used to introduce a factory-made low-fat spread, which has nothing to do with the country and is a blend of milk and vegetable oils. Phrases such as 'a taste of the country', 'full of natural goodness' and 'country style' can give a misleading impression of a natural product.

⇨ Adverts for Milk Tray chocolates show a James Bond-type figure swinging from cliff tops, mountaineering, skiing, and overcoming every obstacle, just to deliver a box of chocolates to a beautiful lady 'and all because the lady loves Milk Tray'. No one took it seriously but they might absorb the underlying message that chocolates make a romantic gift for a lady.

⇨ Glamorous surroundings and elegant people are often used in adverts for luxury goods and help to give a product its 'brand image'. Brand image means the way that people see a certain brand or make of product, its quality, the way it performs and the sort of people who are likely to use it. Glamour, flattery and suggestion are all used to strengthen brand image. Martini ads are noted for their lively sophistication with young attractive people on yachts, water skiing and relaxing in elegant surroundings and people drinking Martini. A strong musical soundtrack reinforces the message: 'Anytime, anyplace, anywhere. There's a wonderful world you can share. It's the bright one, the right one. That's Martini.'

How to read an advert

There are very strict rules about what can and can't be said in an advert. Criminal laws and strong codes of practice mean that what you read is unlikely to be untrue. But with the clever use of suggestion, music, and photography it's quite easy to get a misleading impression. Advertising will only ever tell half the story – the

half the advertiser wants you to know. An advert for a food product might say that it is rich in vitamins, tasty and nutritious – without mentioning that it is high in fat or cholesterol. The language used in an advert can be very important. Here are some examples of phrases which are totally meaningless but which are still persuasive...

⇨ 'helps to combat grease and dirt...' – this doesn't say how effective the product is, how it must be used and whether it is any better than soap and water.

Photo: Herbert Berends

Most TV commercials last for only thirty seconds and so can't give out much information

⇨ 'lasts up to three times longer...' – the 'up to' here means there's no guarantee that the product will last three times longer. And it doesn't tell you what it's being compared with.

⇨ 'probably the best lager in the world...' – this is just a matter of taste and of opinion. A more informative advert would say how it was made, packed and stored and why this made it a better lager.

⇨ 'virtually no maintenance required...' – another way of putting this might be – 'some maintenance is required'. The double negative gives the misleading impression that the item is maintenance-free.

Advertisers vs consumers

Advertisers would say that advertising is a £5,781 million business, employing hundreds of thousands of people.

⇨ Advertising helps businesses

and consumers by providing products which consumers want at economical prices. Advertising increases sales and so manufacturers can step up production and make things more efficiently and cheaply (this is called an economy of scale). Because extra products are being produced more cheaply, the saving can be passed on to the consumer in the form of lower prices.

⇨ Without advertising, all commercial newspapers and radio and TV stations would have to close because they are dependent on advertising for their income. A Sunday newspaper gets 66% of its income from advertising.

⇨ If the only channel for news was state-sponsored, it could lead to a form of censorship of the news and less free speech.

⇨ Consumers would probably support the advertisers in resisting a ban on all advertising. Informative adverts, such as those found in the classified section of any newspaper, are a valuable source of information and, unless they contain information which is wrong, there can be no objection to them.

⇨ Consumers might want more control over persuasive adverts, those sophisticated campaigns run by manufacturers to persuade us to buy brand A rather than B.

⇨ Adverts can be misleading as they show two virtually identical products in a completely different light and give the impression that there are great differences between them. There are dozens of shampoos on the market with prices varying by over 500%. Each brand may have a very similar chemical formula but will have a different brand image, due to the manufacturer's advertising campaign.

⇨ The above information is reprinted with kind permission from Consumer Education. Visit www.consumereducation.org.uk for more information.

© Consumer Education

Advertising and children

Information from the Advertising Standards Authority

Images of children often appear in advertisements, both those designed to sell children's products and those designed to persuade adults to buy anything from car insurance to carpets. Further, it's not only products that are advertised in this way; charities and health agencies regularly use images of neglected and damaged children in their advertising to powerful effect.

The effect of advertising on children and the use and portrayal of children in advertisements are sensitive issues. The advertising standards code are the responsibility of an industry body called the Committee of Advertising Practice (CAP). The codes lay down strict rules on advertising and children. This rule book is used by the Advertising Standards Authority to judge if an ad is acceptable when investigating complaints.

Common issues surrounding children and advertising are:
⇨ Making children desire things they cannot afford or would not be able to use.
⇨ Pester power: encouraging children to pester their parents for advertised products or services.
⇨ Showing children in unsafe or dangerous situations that other kids might emulate.
⇨ Making children feel inferior, especially if they don't buy the products or services shown in the ads.
⇨ Showing children in a sexual way, i.e. wearing make-up and glamorous clothes.
⇨ Advertising soft drinks and high fat / sugar foods to children.

Advertising regulation

CAP and the ASA were established to regulate advertising on a self-regulatory basis, that is to say, the advertising industry taking responsibility itself for laying down rules. The advertising codes for TV, radio and non-broadcast media each have rules on advertising and children. Read the codes on the ASA website or the CAP website. How similar are the rules in the advertising standards code to the BBFC and BBC guidelines on children and media?

For the purposes of judging ads against the advertising codes a child is described as someone under 16 years old. It is recognised, however, that children of different ages are at different stages of development; 6-year-olds, for example, have less experience and life skills than teenagers. So when interpreting the advertising codes, advertisers should remain aware that a child's perception and reaction to an advertisement is influenced by their age, their experience and the context in which an advertisement reaches them.

The scheduling of TV commercials

TV commercials can be particularly appealing to children because of the way they often tell a simple story in a short time frame. Unlike ads in specialist magazines that may be targeted at adults, such as car, home or computer magazines, children may easily see TV commercials during the day. This means the content of ads shown during the day and particularly around children's programmes should be suitable for them. For example, they should not frighten children or make them feel inferior or emulate dangerous activities. The Rules on the Scheduling of Advertising are used to decide when ads should be shown. The ASA can decide if ads can be shown at any time, at times other than around children's programmes (referred to as Ex-Kids), after 7.30pm and after 9pm (known as the Watershed).

Children and food advertising

The ASA has had to look into the issue of how advertisers address children's diets on a number of occasions.

Society is particularly concerned that children's nutritional needs are being met and that they are getting enough exercise.

Advertisements for food aimed at children need to be responsible and the CAP Code states that marketing communications should not actively encourage children to: eat or drink at or near bedtime, eat frequently throughout the day, or replace main meals with confectionery or snack foods.

Child obesity is an issue of national importance in contemporary Britain. Young people are eating foods high in fat and sugar and not exercising enough to work off the calories. Some health professionals believe that this is leading to a national epidemic of children who are overweight and who will have enormous health problems in the future. This is distressing for everyone and is also a major drain on the National Health Service. Many companies, therefore, are attempting to reduce the unhealthy elements in their products and are promoting a healthier way of eating.

Portrayal of children

The portrayal of children in a sexualised manner is the strongest taboo in advertising, according to those questioned in an ASA-commissioned survey into serious offence in non-broadcast advertisements. You can find the report in the research section of the ASA website www.asa.org.uk. All of the 2,000 people questioned thought that this had the potential to cause serious offence.

Respondents were also concerned about the advertising that children might see. 92% of those questioned thought a cautious approach should be taken with poster advertising because children may see it.
February 2007

⇨ The above information is taken from the Advertising Standards Authority's schools and college resource 'Children and Advertising'. For more information or to view the full document, visit www.asa.org.uk
© *Advertising Standards Authority*

Childhood 'dying in spend, spend Britain'

By Sarah Womack, Social Affairs Correspondent

Childhood is under threat from a deluge of marketing and advertising aimed at the young, according to a new report endorsed by the Archbishop of Canterbury.

The impact of the consumer society is now so deep that seven out of 10 three-year-olds recognise the McDonald's logo but only half know their own surname, said Compass, a left-of-centre think-tank.

Children were 'engulfed' by images – sometimes of a sexually suggestive nature – of how they should look and what they should own.

> **The impact of the consumer society is now so deep that seven out of 10 three-year-olds recognise the McDonald's logo but only half know their own surname**

Parents were subverted by the barrage, which 'exploited children's emotional vulnerabilities in the name of profit'.

The average 10-year-old had 'internalised 300 to 400 brands – perhaps 20 times the number of birds in the wild that they could name' and British children are among the most materialistic in the world, ahead of even the Americans, it said.

The report, *Commercialisation of Childhood*, comes amid a national inquiry by the Children's Society into childhood conducted by the Government's unofficial 'happiness tsar' Lord Layard. It reports next year.

Leading figures including Dr Rowan Williams, the Archbishop of Canterbury and patron of the national inquiry, are concerned that rampant marketing is behind rising levels of stress, depression and low self-esteem in children. He said the Compass document was timely and pertinent.

'There is an increasing political and social consensus that something needs to be done to safeguard children from the worst excesses of direct marketing and the pressures of commercialisation,' he said. Compass drew on research from a variety of sources to warn that the style and ubiquity of marketing to children is having a huge and potentially damaging influence.

Female singers 'dress like quintessential male fantasies of teenybopper hookers and sing songs about sex written by middle-aged men', and are marketed to children, it quotes Susan Linn, author of *Consuming Kids*, as saying.

The report includes examples of dolls' sets – the Bratz Secret Date Collection – containing champagne glasses and 'tons of date night accessories'. Vivid Imaginations, distributors of Bratz dolls in the UK, said the brand was marketed at 12-year-olds, although younger girls aspired to own them. A million were sold in Britain last year and Forever Diamondz dolls, with their faux furs and sparkly decorated spray-on jeans, are said to be this Christmas's 'must have' for girls. 'You can't stop younger girls buying them as you can't stop them watching pop videos,' said a spokeswoman.

She said the champagne glasses were 'just glasses that could have squash in them to a child. Only adults would recognise them as champagne glasses.'

One American commentator has said Bratz dolls appear sexual – 'like pole dancers on their way to a gentlemen's club'. But the spokeswoman said: 'A consumer psychologist at Exeter University has said that's an adult's perspective. To a girl, it's a pretty doll and they are buying into fashion dolls. Adults are over intellectualising.'

Sue Palmer, a former head teacher and author of *Toxic Childhood*, said children's clothing was being designed in overtly adult styles to expose a lot of flesh.

Today's report says the bombardment of children with messages of what is cool pits children against each other and their parents.

Wal-Mart, for example, has taken the concept of Santa's list to a new level. On its website, Toyland, it asks children to pick items they would like from a conveyor belt and to enter their parents' email addresses so the list can be sent on and the company can 'help pester your parents'.

A Wal-Mart spokesman said: 'Kids have been writing lists for Christmas presents for hundreds of years. All we've done is put a modern slant on the tradition.'

The Compass report concludes: 'Millions of pounds are spent conditioning children to become young consumers. Who is forming our children – parents, guardians, friends, families, teachers, community workers – or an army of psychologists, branding gurus, marketing experts, advertisers who are spending billions to shape young minds in the name of profit? Can children be children before they are consumers?'

Consuming passions

Shopping

The report points out that the child-orientated market in the UK is now worth £30 billion.

By the age of 10, 78 per cent of children say they 'enjoy shopping'.

Research by the National Consumer Council says that the average 10-year-old has 'internalised 300 to 400 brands – perhaps 20 times the number of birds in the wild that they could name'.

Michael Brody, of the American Academy of Child and Adolescent Psychiatry, said the commercialisation of children was having serious consequences.

He said story-telling was once the essence of play, with toys as catalysts.

But today's toys, with their overt commercial links, were effectively 'story blockers'.

TV advertising

The average child in the UK, US and Australia sees between 20,000 and 40,000 television advertisements a year.

Adults are generally able to detect methods that are being employed to sell them something. Children do not usually develop that capacity until the age of 11 or 12. Up to the age of eight, children are not at all aware of the marketers' intent.

Marketing experts say 'product placements' may get under the radar of even older children (13 years and above) when it is well done.

According to a website that counts brand references in films, Brandchannel.com, this year's *Pink Panther* film (rated PG in the UK) featured more than 30 brands, including Adidas, TGI Friday and Virgin.

Branding

The report highlights what it regards as a significant warning from America – a trend among parents to name newborn children after global brands.

By the age of 10, 78 per cent of children say they 'enjoy shopping'

Prof Cleveland Evans of Bellevue University in Nebraska came across the trend when surveying the 2,000 US social security records. He found 300 girls called Armani, six boys named after Courvoisier cognac, girls called L'Oreal and one boy named after sports channel ESPN.

Martin Lindstrom, a marketing guru, said that 'as formal religion in the Western world continues to erode, brands move in to fill the vacuum'.

A mother's lament

'I have lost count of the number of tantrums I have had in Asda because I won't let the girls have a cereal just for the free gift.

'I feel like I have to keep saying no, because obviously with two children and not working, I just haven't got the money.

'And they want this and they want that and I'm forever going "no, no, no" and I wonder what the children must think of me – "Oh, I hate mum. She never buys me anything". It does get really upsetting sometimes.

'I need to ask if the advertising industry is comfortable spending millions of pounds targeting children direct and then saying it's down to mum and dad to stand up to them.'

The report noted that particular anxiety centred on the design of girls' clothing to include overtly adult styles, particularly those that exposed a lot of flesh.

Pester power

The report quotes the National Consumer Council, saying British children are more consumer-orientated than their American counterparts.

They are more brand aware and less satisfied than US children with what they have to spend.

Adolescents who report higher levels of family stress are also more likely to associate material possessions with happiness. The report says pester power works so well because parents are worried about their children's experiences in the school playground. And some children have shown they will do anything to fit in.

Materialism has been shown to contribute to competitiveness and aggression in boys, 'so it is not surprising that bullying remains a big problem in schools'.

13 December 2006

© *Telegraph Group Limited, London 2007*

Debt and young people

Percentage of clients counselled by the Consumer Credit Counselling Service in each age group, by year.

Age group	2002	2003	2004	2005
Under 25	5.9	10.3	15.2	12.6
25-39	52.1	48.7	46.7	46.3
40-59	37.8	36.0	33.5	36.3
60 and over	4.3	5.0	4.6	4.9

Source: Consumer Credit Counselling Service.

Shopping addiction

Information from the Priory Group

People use what is called retail therapy as a way of enjoying themselves. They normally buy items for which they have a need or have developed a desire for. Compulsive or addictive shopping is not like that, it is a form of behaviour designed to avoid unpleasant reality, and is accompanied by a high which causes the sufferer to lose control and buy many items for which they have no need. The adrenalin rush, the fantasy which surrounds the episode and everything which precedes the actual spending spree all add to the sense of unreality which brings a false sense of freedom from life's problems.

> **Compulsive or addictive shopping is not like [retail therapy], it is a form of behaviour designed to avoid unpleasant reality, and is accompanied by a high which causes the sufferer to lose control**

How common is it?

It is difficult to ascertain the full extent of this problem as statistics have not been compiled, although it is known that more people are identifying this as a problem and seeking professional help.

How do I know if I have it?

As with all addictions, the resulting overwhelming sense of shame, remorse and guilt accompanied by feelings of hopelessness and helplessness, lead to despair. Often the remedy for the despair is more addictive behaviour resulting in more self-destructive feelings. The

PRIORY

consequences of shopping addiction are obvious: high levels of debt, fear of discovery and retribution leading to more denial and desperate acts to cover up the behaviour. For those closely connected to the sufferer life becomes frightening and unpredictable with a growing sense of uselessness and the belief that the sufferer is deliberately causing chaos and a feeling of desperation sets in. Complete the questionnaire on the Priory Group website to help you decide if you have a problem.

Can it be cured?

Many sufferers are multi-addicted, often abusing prescribed drugs or alcohol in addition to the compulsive spending. The despair can be ended through successful treatment and people can be restored to normal life. As with other addictions, success follows an honest admission of the problem and the seeking of help from others.

⇨ The above information is reprinted with kind permission from the Priory Group. Visit www.addictions.co.uk for more information.

© *Priory Group*

Men are shopaholics too, say psychologists

⇨ *US study finds sexes almost equally vulnerable*
⇨ *Compulsive buyers often young and on low incomes*

Shopaholics are almost as likely to be men as they are women, according to a study published by psychologists today. The report overturns the widespread view that binge buying is a predominantly female pursuit, and claims more than one in 20 of adults are prone to compulsive spending sprees.

Studies have suggested 90% of shopaholics are women, but in the latest study psychologists found the difference was almost negligible, with the disorder affecting 6% of women and 5.5% of men

Known to psychologists as compulsive buying disorder, people who binge-buy experience waves of irresistible and often senseless urges to shop. They are often left with bundles of unwanted clothes and other items and rack up sizeable debts from frequent shopping bonanzas. The consequences can be severe, leading to bankruptcy, divorce, embezzlement and even suicide attempts.

Previous studies have suggested 90% of shopaholics are women, but in the latest study psychologists found the difference was almost negligible, with the disorder affecting 6% of women and 5.5% of men. Writing in the *American Journal of Psychiatry*, a team lead by Lorrin Koran, an expert in psychiatry and behaviour at Stanford University in California, claims: 'The widespread opinion that most compulsive buyers are women may be wrong.'

By Ian Sample, Science Correspondent

The scientists conducted a telephone survey of 2,513 adults from randomly selected households and asked about buying attitudes and behaviour. The similarity between the sexes came as a huge surprise, said Dr Koran. 'The difference that we observed between the prevalence in women and men is quite small and contrasts with the marked difference reported in clinical trials, in which women constituted 80%-95% of the participants,' he said. The study revealed that compulsive buyers tended to be younger, on low incomes, and four times as likely as others to make only the minimum payment on credit card balances.

The finding adds to recent research that suggests compulsive shopping is a form of obsessive-compulsive disorder that affects men and women equally, although men are less likely to seek help for it.

'A lot of binge buying seems to be driven by feelings of unrelenting perfectionism. People feel incomplete without particular items and believe that having it will make them look nicer, smell nicer, be more appealing,' said Helen Nightingale, a clinical psychologist at the Priory hospital in Manchester. The problem is exacerbated by media images of perfect, unattainable lifestyles.

Compulsive buying among women may be more conspicuous, with vast sums being spent on make-up and clothes. Among men, the disorder is more likely to lead to an amassing of gadgets, or sprees on cars and sporting equipment, Dr Nightingale added. Although a spending spree might give very temporary relief to urges, overspending on unnecessary items usually drives anxiety levels up, causing a vicious circle of buying and remorse.

Although common, the condition can be treated using cognitive behaviour therapy, a psychological technique that helps patients to adjust their outlook on life and lower anxiety levels. 'Compulsive buying leads to serious psychological, financial and family problems, including depression, overwhelming debt and the breakup of relationships,' said Dr Koran. 'People don't realise the extent of damage it does to the sufferer.'

30 September 2006

UK is Europe's number one online retail market

Internet retail sales in the UK have overtaken those in Germany, as the UK is crowned 'king of the clicks'

Latest research from Mintel shows that although Germany is the largest economy in Europe, Internet retail sales in the UK (9.79bn Euros) stood some 80 million Euros ahead of Germany (9.71bn Euros) last year, making the UK Europe's* biggest online retail market. France, in third position, followed a considerable way behind with 2005 sales of just 6.50bn Euros.

In 2005 on-line retail sales in the UK, Germany and France collectively made up almost two-thirds (65%) of the 40.2bn Euro European e-commerce market

In 2005 online retail sales in the UK, Germany and France collectively made up almost two-thirds (65%) of the 40.2bn Euro European* e-commerce market. Overall, this market has grown at a phenomenal rate – up an impressive 51% on the 26.6bn Euros of 2004 – and yet the sector still only amounted to 2% of total European retail sales. However, Mintel estimates show that this market is expected to grow by a further 186% between 2005 and 2010. With sales forecast to reach some 115bn Euros, e-commerce is set to increase its share of total European retail sales from 2% to nearer 5% over this five-year period.

'The business to consumer e-commerce sector has come of age and is gaining consumer acceptance as a "normal" retail sales channel. Mintel is confident that online sales

MINTeL

of goods will grow strongly over the next few years as this channel matures. But physical shops will not sit back and watch their trade drain away, they will respond by making the physical shopping experience more enjoyable and rewarding with much better interaction from informed and trained staff,' comments Neil Mason, senior retail analyst at Mintel.

According to Mintel's June 2006 Internet Quarterly report almost two in three (65%) adults now have access to the Internet, rising to some 80% amongst those who work. Greater competition among UK broadband providers has led to falling prices and faster Internet speeds, which has ultimately been the major driver of growth in terms of Internet penetration in the last 12 months. When it comes to buying online, half (50%) of Internet users have bought from the site they were browsing. Meanwhile, 30% bought not from the site they were browsing but from the site owner's bricks and mortar store, up from just one in four (24%) back at the start of 2004, showing a rising level of loyalty amongst consumers.

France growing fastest

By 2010 the UK, France and Germany will each have online retail sales worth over 18bn Euros. Of the three countries France will experience the greatest growth, with retail sales increasing just over 200% between

2005 and 2010 to reach 19.60bn Euros. The UK will remain the largest market growing 102% to an impressive 19.80bn Euros. Although Germany will experience the slowest growth over this five-year period, online retail sales are still expected to increase by 93% to reach 18.74bn Euros.

'France has a relatively immature e-commerce market, due to Minitel and to the French love affair with going out regularly to physical shops for fresh produce or for their clothes. The French market is a lot smaller than that of Germany and the UK and as such has much greater potential for growth in coming years. This leads us to forecast relatively rapid increases in e-commerce sales now that the Internet is an accepted part of French life. When it comes to Germany, Mintel believes that while the general economy will expand it will take a while for the benefits to feed through to consumer expenditure and to retail sales both online and on the high street, meaning that Intenet retails sales are set to resume only modest growth across the current decade,' comments Neil Mason.

Italy (13.24bn Euros) and Spain (10.88bn Euros) complete the top five Internet markets for 2010, with each e-commerce market in the remaining 14 European countries coming in at just 4bn Euros or under.

The demise of 'Big Book' mail order

Much e-commerce growth will be derived from mail order companies switching business from the relatively expensive processing of paper orders from traditional catalogues to virtually free processing of Internet orders. This format will lead ultimately to the demise of traditional big book catalogues as they become progressively more uneconomic to operate.

Growth will of course be down to the Internet retailers themselves as they need to persuade more of us to buy more on the Internet. In part this will be through reassuring consumers in areas like credit card payment security and also ensuring that deliveries and returns operate smoothly and at minimal cost. More retailers will start trading online and this widening choice will encourage greater spending. More food retailers will offer Internet home delivery services and this will play a big part in expanding the sector – although Mintel expects that discount-focused Germany will lag behind other countries in this aspect of online selling.

* For the purpose of this report we have covered 19 European countries. These are: UK, France, Italy, Germany, Spain, Netherlands, Ireland, Portugal, Greece, Austria, Switzerland, Belgium, Norway, Denmark, Sweden, Finland, Czech Republic, Hungary and Poland

About Mintel

Mintel is a worldwide leader of competitive media, product and consumer intelligence. For more than 35 years, Mintel has provided key insight into leading global trends. With offices in Chicago, London, Belfast and Sydney, Mintel's innovative product line provides unique data that has a direct impact on client success. For more information on Mintel, please visit their website at www.mintel.com.
March 2006

⇨ The above information is reprinted with kind permission from Mintel. Visit www.mintel.com for more information.

© Mintel

Women and online shopping

Why women won't shop online till it includes lunch with friends

Men are increasingly using the internet for their shopping needs while women still favour high street stores, research reveals.

A study found that 14 per cent of men spent more than £2,000 online last year, but only five per cent of women

---

While the growth of online shopping shows no sign of slowing, it is predominantly being driven by men. A study found that 14 per cent of men spent more than £2,000 online last year, but only five per cent of women.

The explanation is that women see shopping as a social experience, which the internet does not provide, and like to see what they are buying before parting with their cash, experts said yesterday.

Cynthia McVey, a psychologist at Glasgow Caledonia University, said: 'Stereotypes are true – many men don't like shopping on the high

---

By James OrrLast

---

street. If they need something they will go online, have a look at it, assume it will be okay and buy it.

'A woman, however, will "want to feel the fabric". For them, shopping is often more of a social event. They like to go with their friends, get advice from them before buying and catch up over lunch.'

The online survey by service provider Affinity Planet asked more than 3,000 adults about buying goods online. It found that 55 per cent of men, but 40 per cent of women, bought products priced between £100 and £500, and that 36 per cent of women but 20 per cent of men said it was vital to have heard of a retailer or brand before buying online.

Prof Barrie Gunter at the University of Leicester said: 'For some women, shopping is about going out and being within the retail environment. More than men, they like to have direct contact with the merchandise they are going to purchase.'

Online shopping grew by 32 per cent in 2005, prompting fears of the demise of high street stores, and is expected to rise by 36 per cent this

year. Last year, according to internet retail body IMRG, about 24 million British customers bought online, spending a total of £19.2 billion. Four out of five shoppers now buy books, music, television and film products online.
11 March 2006

© *Telegraph Group Limited, London 2007*

Consumer rights

We all occasionally blow our pay cheques on that thing we really 'had to have' only to discover it wasn't all that great after all. Luckily, you are protected by consumer rights with everything you buy

Your rights

You have the right to expect certain standards in the goods you buy. The law says that goods must be:

⇨ Of satisfactory quality – This covers, for example, the appearance and finish of goods, their safety and durability. Goods must be free from defects, usually even minor ones, except when they have been brought to your attention by the seller. For example, if the goods are said to be shop soiled or you examined the goods and should have noticed the defects;

⇨ Fit for their purposes, including any particular purpose mentioned by you to the seller – If you tell the seller that you want boots fit for mountain climbing, that is what you should get;

⇨ As described – On the package or display sign, or by the seller. If you are told that a jumper is 100% wool it should not turn out to have acrylic in it.

These are your statutory rights. All goods bought or hired from a trader – from a shop, street market, catalogue or doorstep seller – are covered by these rights. This includes goods bought in sales.

If things go wrong

If there is something wrong with goods you have bought, tell the seller as soon as you can. If you cannot get back to the shop quickly, telephone to explain the problem.

If you tell the seller promptly that the goods are faulty and you do not want them, you should be able to get your money back. You may be offered a replacement, free repair or credit note but you do not have to accept. If you do accept a credit note and cannot find anything else you want, you are unlikely to be able to exchange it for cash later on. If you take goods back straight away and the seller tries to repair them and fails, you still have the same right to reject that you had when you agreed to the repair.

Do not delay in examining what you have bought or in telling the seller about a fault. You are entitled to a reasonable time to examine goods before you are considered in law to have accepted them.

Photo: Steve Woods

What is reasonable depends on all the circumstances, but normally you can at least take your purchase home and try it out. If you sign an acceptance note when you receive goods, you still have a reasonable time to examine them afterwards.

If you do not complain promptly, you may not be able to reject (that is, refuse to accept) the goods, and you may lose your right to a full refund. The trader may offer to have, or to pay for, the goods to be repaired. If the goods cannot be repaired you are entitled to damages, which may be the cost of a replacement.

If you receive goods as a present and they turn out to be faulty, it is up to the person who bought them to return the goods to the seller. The buyer has the contract with the seller. Many shops, however, will deal with your complaint providing you have some proof of purchase.

You are not legally obliged to return faulty goods to the seller at your own expense. If an item would be difficult or expensive to return because, for example, it is bulky, ask the seller to collect it. This does not apply if you have had the goods for some time, or you got them as a present.

You may be able to claim compensation if you suffer loss because of faulty goods. For example, if clothes are damaged by a faulty iron.

You do not need a receipt to complain about faulty goods, although it is useful evidence of when and where the purchase was made.

You are not entitled to anything if you:

⇨ examined the goods when you bought them and should have seen the fault;

⇨ were told about the fault;

⇨ simply change your mind;

⇨ made a mistake when you bought the goods;

⇨ did the damage yourself.

But even in these circumstances, many shops will help out of goodwill.

⇨ The above information is reprinted with kind permission from TheSite.org. Visit www.thesite.org for more information.

© TheSite.org

Your rights

Deposits

Think twice about paying a deposit because if the firm goes out of business you could get little or nothing back. The best course is not to pay anything in advance unless you have to. Sometimes it's probably unavoidable – with home improvements, for example, or made-to-measure goods.

Try not to pay a deposit to a firm you know little or nothing about, particularly if the address consists simply of a box number and post code. Try to find out something about the firm: if it's local it should be listed in the phone book. Check if it belongs to a trade association which runs a scheme to protect prepayments.

Tips:
- ⇨ If you do pay anything in advance make sure you get a receipt showing the company's name and address.
- ⇨ Check whether deposits are returnable and, if so, in precisely what circumstances, because if you do pay a deposit and then cancel the order, the firm could claim it is entitled to keep the deposit.

If you use a credit card to pay a deposit for goods or services costing more than £100, you may have more protection.

If you use certain other types of credit such as a linked credit agreement (in which the trader, from whom you are buying goods or services, agrees to arrange your loan with a finance company), any deposit you pay is refundable if the credit agreement is not accepted by the finance company.

Untrue claims

It's a criminal offence for a trader to write or say something untrue about goods or (in some circumstances) services. For example, if a car is said to have only 20,000 miles on the clock or a dry cleaners offers a 24-hour service, these statements must be true.

Estimates and quotations

An informed guess is an estimate – a rough price. But if you agree to a fixed price, this is a quotation – a fixed price is binding whatever it is called. Make sure you know which you are getting and ask for the figures to be put in writing. Check whether the prices quoted include VAT.

If you think you've been misled, contact Consumer Direct for advice.

Buying on credit

If a trader has an arrangement with a credit card or finance company that allows you to pay by credit (for goods that cost more than £100) you may have extra protection because the credit card or finance company may also be liable for any claim you have against the trader.

For example, if the goods are not delivered or are not what you ordered, or a holiday was wrongly described or you didn't get what you paid for, you might be able to claim from the credit card or finance company.

Although it's a good idea to approach the trader first, you can make a claim against the credit card issuer or finance company without doing this. Contact Consumer Direct for advice prior to making a claim.

Be aware – you don't have these rights if you pay with a debit card or a charge card.

Goods on order from a shop

If you order something that's not in stock or has to be delivered, like a new washing machine, you may agree a delivery date. Get this in writing because if the goods don't arrive on time, you can refuse to accept them.

Even if you don't ask for an estimated delivery date, the seller must still deliver within a reasonable time. If you think you've waited long enough, tell the seller that you want a full refund unless the item arrives within a certain period (14 days might be reasonable).

Be aware – if you do agree at this point to wait longer you cannot cancel during that time.

When you order something, you and the seller should agree a fixed price. You might agree that if the cost of the goods goes up before delivery, you'll pay the increase. In some instances the cost might not be known. Whatever the situation, make sure you know where you stand – preferably in writing.

Guarantees

Guarantees give you additional rights which could be a useful back-up if you have to complain. Guarantees should be clear, unambiguous and available for you to see before you make a purchase.

With some goods you may have a manufacturer's guarantee. Make sure, where there is a registration card for return to the manufacturer, that the seller has filled in details of the purchase – otherwise the card might not be valid.

For the guarantee to be effective, you might need to ensure that you return the registration card to a stated address. Make sure you keep the documentation supplied with the goods that tells you how to make a claim under the guarantee.

Don't choose a firm just because it guarantees its services. A 10-year guarantee for a new house extension may be worthless if the firm goes out of business. Insurance-backed guarantee schemes, however, are available through some trade associations to cover building work. For long-term schemes make sure that the insurance covers the same period as the guarantee.

Guarantees give you additional rights which could be a useful back-up if you have to complain. Guarantees should be clear, unambiguous and available for you to see before you make a purchase

---

Be aware – guarantees cannot be legally used to exclude or limit a shop's or dealer's liability for selling goods that are defective or do not correspond with their description.

Extended warranties

If you buy goods such as a television, cooker or washing machine, you might be offered an extended guarantee or warranty – but you might have to pay extra for this. Think carefully about the value for money offered by an extended warranty because it is likely to be expensive compared with the amount you would normally pay out in repair costs.

Some people forget that the goods they buy new have a manufacturer's guarantee that usually lasts for one year, so there is no need to buy an extended warranty when you buy the goods.

If you decide that you would like a warranty, you do not have to buy one at the shop where you bought the

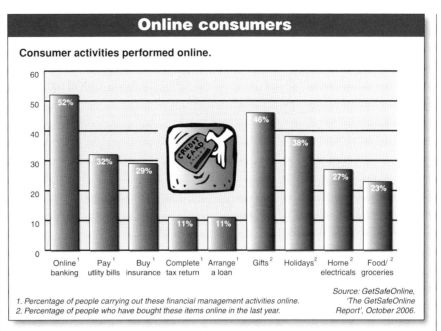

Online consumers

Consumer activities performed online.

Source: GetSafeOnline, 'The GetSafeOnline Report', October 2006.

1. Percentage of people carrying out these financial management activities online.
2. Percentage of people who have bought these items online in the last year.

goods. There are a number of firms – including insurance companies and the manufacturers themselves – that sell extended warranties on everyday household goods, from toasters to computers. In some cases, they may be cheaper and more comprehensive than retailers' extended warranties. It is now also possible to buy warranties that cover a number of appliances, such as all the electrical equipment in your kitchen. So it is certainly a good idea to shop around for some quotes before signing up to a warranty.

The law also requires retailers to provide certain information on warranties they are selling, and you may get rights to cancel your extended warranty if you choose to do so. Contact Consumer Direct for advice.

Cashbacks

A number of extended warranties are now sold on a 'cashback' basis. With these, your premium is returned in full if you have not made a claim for a fixed period – usually five years. If you buy this type of warranty and do not make a claim, it is your responsibility to take steps to recover the premium when the time is up. Make sure you read the terms very carefully. You may only be given a short time in which to register your cashback status after signing the warranty, and you are only allowed a few weeks in which to ask for return of the premium after the five years have passed. Of course you have to remember to do this, and keep the documents safe in the meantime.

Tips:

⇨ Remember – cashback schemes are only as good as the company providing them. If the company goes out of business, you may not receive any cashback.

⇨ Before you sign it, check the wording carefully to see what the warranty does and does not cover.

⇨ Check the procedures for making a claim. Will the warranty pay for repairs up front or will you have to pay first and then claim the money back afterwards?

⇨ Always keep details of any guarantee or warranty with your original receipt and any service or repair documents. Make a note of serial numbers for future reference.

Exclusion clauses

Some traders might try to escape their responsibilities under contracts by using exclusion clauses, for instance by saying that they accept no liability for loss or damage. If an exclusion clause is unfair it is legally void and cannot be used against you.

Generally, only a court can decide if a contract term is unfair. But any exclusion of liability, whether in a contract term or on a notice, is always void if it is used for the purpose of evading liability for death or personal injury caused by negligence. Also, a trader selling goods cannot exclude liability for a breach of your statutory rights – for instance by displaying a sign saying: 'no refunds given'. An attempt to do this is an offence.

Similar statements about services – for example: 'no responsibility for loss or damage to garments, however caused' on the back of a dry cleaning ticket – are not illegal. But such terms are not enforceable if a court finds them unfair. We have more information about unfair terms in contracts.

Doorstep selling

When a seller calls on you, do not sign or commit yourself to anything until you've had time to think things over and compare prices with other companies. The seller might offer you a special discount, a free gift or other incentive if you sign on the spot. Do not feel pressured by this kind of offer.

Tips:
⇨ Do not sign anything until you've read the agreement very carefully and if there's anything you don't understand, ask.
⇨ If you're not happy with the explanation, get the agreement checked out by someone in whom you have confidence, or by a consumer adviser.
⇨ Keep a copy of anything you sign.
⇨ If the value of the goods is over £35, you may have rights to cancel the contract. Contact Consumer Direct for advice.

Buying at auctions

Take care if you buy at an auction. Auctioneers, unlike other sellers, may be able to refuse to accept responsibility for the quality of the goods they auction:
⇨ Look out for exclusion clauses.
⇨ Read notices and catalogues carefully.
⇨ Note any conditions of sale, such as buyers' premium, terms and method of payment, deposits and time limits for the removal of goods.

Be aware – you can't back out of the deal once the hammer has fallen.

If you buy privately – perhaps through a classified ad in the local paper – you have fewer rights than when you buy from a trader. The general rule is 'buyer beware'

Buying second-hand goods

You have the same rights as when buying new ones, but you must take into account that second-hand will not be of the same quality as brand new. You can, however, still claim your money back or the cost of repairs if the goods are faulty, unless the faults are matter of the wear and tear to be expected with second-hand goods, or were pointed out to you, or were obvious when you agreed to buy the goods. Examine goods carefully before you buy.

Private sales

If you buy privately – perhaps through a classified ad in the local paper – you have fewer rights than when you buy from a trader. The general rule is 'buyer beware'.

Privately-bought goods do not have to be free of faults, but they must be 'as described'. For example, a leather coat should not be plastic, and full-length curtains must not be half-length.

If the seller says anything misleading about the condition of the goods, and you buy on the basis of what is said, then you will be able to seek a legal remedy if the goods turn out differently. However, this could be difficult to prove.

Tips:
⇨ Take someone with you to act as a witness to any conversations.
⇨ Ask for a written description of the goods.

Beware of traders posing as private sellers, perhaps at a car boot sale or through a small ad. This practice is illegal and takes advantage of the fact that you have fewer rights when you buy from a private seller.

If you do suspect the seller is a trader – for example, you've seen lots of small ads with the same phone number or the seller insists on meeting you at your home – contact Consumer Direct.

Telephone sales

Many companies use the phone to promote their goods and services. If you'd like to reduce the number of sales calls you receive, contact your telephone company and ask to register with the Telephone Preference Service. Once you've registered it is an offence for a company to make unsolicited calls to you. If calls still keep coming in, you can take up your complaint with the industry regulator Ofcom.

⇨ The above information is reprinted with kind permission from Consumer Direct. Visit www.consumerdirect.gov.uk for more information.

© Crown copyright

CONSUME NOW...   ...PAY LATER

Changes to consumer rights

Government announces major overhaul of consumer rights

By Miles Brignall

The government has announced a major overhaul of consumer rights in the UK with the formation of a new super-body to ensure consumers' interests are better represented.

Consumer minister Ian McCartney announced that a new organisation, to be called Consumer Voice, will replace the National Consumer Council, Energywatch and Postwatch.

> **The government has announced a major overhaul of consumer rights in the UK with the formation of a new super-body to ensure consumers' interests are better represented**

He said the new body would act as a 'powerful and effective advocate' for consumers.

Today's announcement ends a consultation process started in January, although it will be around two years before the body opens its doors to its first customers.

Mr McCartney said Consumer Voice will represent the interests of consumers across a range of markets and have the 'responsibility and authority to voice the concerns of all UK consumers'.

It will also extend the redress scheme to resolve complaints and 'to award compensation to consumers where warranted'.

'We want to give people an effective system of representation and redress that is easily accessible and offers the best possible all-round protection,' he said. 'In the end, this is about getting people a better deal for their money and protecting them from being ripped off.'

A spokesman said the body plans to build on the success of Consumer Direct, the existing, phone-based consumer advice service, which recently took its 2,000,000th phone call. He said it will have a number of permanent offices throughout England, Scotland and Wales.

The new body will be welcomed by consumers, particularly those who have complained to Energywatch about their gas or electricity supplier.

Many have found that Energywatch had no powers to intervene following a dispute over a bill even though their case was proven.

Last November, Energywatch and Postwatch were described by the House of Commons public accounts committee as 'performing feebly'. MPs found that hardly anybody had heard of either body.

However, there is one notable omission. A Department of Trade and Industry spokesman said that Consumer Voice will not cover the telecoms and broadband sector as originally proposed. Complaints about broadband providers are currently running at record levels, although the body which oversees the market, Ofcom, rarely intervenes on consumers' behalf.

Louise Hanson, head of campaigns at the private consumer group Which? said: 'Which? broadly welcomes the move to consolidate a number of bodies that represent the consumer interest and we are particularly pleased to see that measures for redress have been included to help consumers when things go wrong. However, we hope that the merging of several consumer interest organisations will not see a drop in resourcing for essential consumer protection.'

Mr McCartney said the government was 'committed to taking forward work to make this happen without delay'. 'Legislation will be required to deliver the new model for consumer representation and redress, and we intend to bring this before parliament as soon as possible.'

17 October 2006

Using credit wisely

Information from the Consumer Credit Counselling Service

Personal loans

There are a number of ways to obtain a personal loan, over the Internet, replying to a letter received in the post offering credit, general advertisements or a visit to your local bank branch. Shop around and look for the best rate of interest and bear in mind that the longer the term of the loan the more you will pay.

Most people fall into debt through no fault of their own

Overdrafts

If you need to temporarily overdraw, it is essential that you get approval from your bank before you do so, to avoid higher interest rates and charges for unauthorised lending – typically £25.

Credit cards

Even though they are very convenient they promote the feeling that you are not actually paying money for something you buy on a credit card. This means you can spend what you like, when you like as long as you do not exceed the agreed credit limit. However, as you approach your agreed limit, you may find that the credit card company informs you that your credit limit has been raised substantially, instead of warning you that you are nearing the limit.

If you do not pay off the balance in full each month, you will be charged interest. As time goes by, you will be paying less of what you borrowed and more of the interest as well as being charged interest on the interest allocated to your account in the previous month. Therefore after a period of time a large amount of what you owe will be accumulated interest.

Store cards

Store cards work in the same way as credit cards but usually attract a higher rate of interest. Unless you receive other valuable benefits from having a store card, you would most likely gain from using a credit card instead.

Interest-free credit

Before signing an interest free agreement, make sure it is exactly that. It is possible to obtain interest-free goods where the total value of the item you are buying is split over a period of time and you only repay the value of the goods. However, some agreements have an interest-free period only for a short time and then revert to interest bearing. To be sure, it is best to ask for a quote for the total amount repayable before signing.

Hire purchase

The main difference between other forms of borrowing and hire purchase is that with other forms of borrowing the goods belong to you straight away, whereas with HP they become legally yours only when you have finished paying for them. If for some reason you stop paying for the goods, they can be repossessed if you have paid less than one-third of the total or you can be taken to court to pay the balance. This form of credit is usually more expensive than for example a loan from your bank, also if your circumstances change for the worse during the agreement, you may lose both your goods and the money you have already paid.

Catalogues

Many people who buy goods through catalogues pay for the items they purchase on a monthly basis. The risk with a catalogue is that during the time you're paying for the items you already have, a new catalogue will arrive and you will be tempted to buy items you don't really need.

Secured and unsecured loans

One of the main factors in determining the rate of interest you will be charged when you borrow is whether your loan is secured against one of your assets – usually an item of significant value e.g. your house. If you fail to repay, the asset can be forcibly repossessed by the lender or at least they can make you sell the asset so that the amount can be reclaimed.

A secured loan is when you offer such an asset as security to the lending organisation. The advantage here is that you will pay a much lower rate of interest than with an unsecured loan. However, when balancing this out against the fact that you may lose your home if you fail to repay, the disadvantages can be huge.

Think before taking on new commitments

Most people fall into debt through no fault of their own – often as a result of redundancy, illness or relationship breakdown et cetera. But it may be that you simply took on more credit card borrowing or interest-free loans than you could afford to repay. If so, resolve to do things differently in future. Having an up-to-date budget showing your income and expenditure will show what money you have available. Check carefully to ensure that any new commitment really is affordable before you sign up for it.

Better still, try to save up for the things you would like to have. Don't buy on impulse.

When it comes to the wise use of credit, being able to afford the repayments is not the only consideration. It is also important to match the repayment period to the 'useful life' of the thing you are buying. For example, if you are taking out a loan for a holiday, you don't want to be paying for it in 3 years' time!

⇨ The above information is reprinted with kind permission from the Consumer Credit Counselling Service. Visit www.cccs.co.uk for more information.

© Consumer Credit Counselling Service

Rise in problem debt

Citizens' Advice Bureaux report steep rise in debt problems

Citizens' Advice Bureaux are reporting a sharp rise in the number of serious debt problems being brought to them. Figures released today by national umbrella charity Citizens' Advice show that their bureau network in England and Wales advised on 1.4 million debt problems in the year 2005/06, an increase of 11% on the previous year.

One in five of all CAB clients needed advice on debt problems. The Citizens' Advice Bureau network is already the largest single provider of free, independent and expert debt advice in the UK.

Consumer credit debt – including problems with credit cards, store cards and charge cards, unsecured personal loans, bank and building society overdrafts. catalogue and mail order debts – remains the biggest problem area, accounting for 824,000 enquiries. The number of consumer credit debt enquiries has more than doubled in the last eight years.

But housing debt, including problems with mortgage, secured loans and rent arrears, was one of the fastest growing problem areas, up by 20% on the previous year. Of the 127,000 housing debt problems brought to Citizens' Advice Bureaux nearly 10,000 concerned threatened repossession and 2,000 concerned actual repossession or eviction. These figures bear out the findings of an NOP survey for Citizens' Advice published in September showing that some 770,000 people had missed at least one mortgage payment in the previous twelve months.

Council tax debt problems handled by bureaux went up by almost half (46%) to 89,000, and utilities debt problems (gas, electricity, telephone and water) were up by 19% to 90,000. Recent big hikes in fuel prices make it likely that these problems will continue to grow.

Bankruptcy accounted for 65,000 of the debt problems handled by Citizens' Advice Bureaux.

Citizens' Advice Chief Executive David Harker said:

'Our debt enquiry figures are deeply worrying. They suggest that a growing number of people are getting deeper into unmanageable debt it will be difficult to recover from. Many of our clients already face a lifetime of debt and research we published in May found it will take them an average of 77 years to pay off the money they owe at a rate they can afford.'

Consumer credit debt remains the biggest problem area, accounting for 824,000 enquiries. The number of consumer credit debt enquiries has more than doubled in the last eight years

---

'We are particularly concerned by the sharp rise in enquiries from people getting behind with mortgage payments and having trouble paying council tax, gas and electricity bills, at a time when court action that can lead to repossession is on the increase, and fuel prices are rising steeply. This is likely to lead to more people than ever experiencing the sort of serious debt problems our advisers are already seeing day in day out.'

Citizens' Advice received £33 million of DTI-administered funding from the Financial Inclusion Fund in April 2006 to increase the availability of face-to-face debt advice to financially excluded clients in deprived communities. This involves recruiting and training 370 new debt advisers within an 18-month period. At the start of October 2006 there were 233 new debt advisers already recruited.

David Harker said, 'Having more debt advisers will enable local bureaux to see people quickly and act at an earlier stage to stop their debts from increasing. However, our evidence shows a clear need for more responsible lending. There are still too many cases where clients should not have been given the levels of credit they have received. Lenders need to do more to ensure every person's circumstances and their ability to sustain payments are fully taken on board when lending. We also want to see all creditors taking steps to help people manage their debt problems.'

7 November 2006

⇨ Citizens' Advice, Nov 2006. Reprinted with permission. Information and advice can be found at www.adviceguide.org.uk

© *Citizens' Advice Bureaux*

Facts and figures

This article provides you with facts and figures about different sectors of the industry, such as the mortgage market, debt, personal spending, students and savings

Total UK personal debt

⇨ Britain's personal debt is increasing by £1 million every four minutes.

⇨ Average household debt in the UK is £7,754 (excluding mortgages) and £48,209 including mortgages.

⇨ At the end of April 2006, the total UK personal debt was £1,191 bn. The growth rate remains strong at 10.2% for the previous 12 months which equates to an increase of £100bn.

⇨ Average owed by every UK adult is £25,545 (including mortgages).

Economy

According to Office for National Statistics data, Britain's economy grew 0.8% in April, May and June 2006, pushing the annual rate up to 2.6%.

According to the Office for National Statistics, in 2006 UK retail sales grew 2.1% in three months to June from the same period a year earlier. This growth is said to be driven by sales of food and drink during the World Cup.

Plastic cards

⇨ According to APACS, a record £151 billion was spent on credit and debit cards in the first half of 2006.

⇨ In 2005, there were 141.6 million payment cards in issue – 69.9 million credit cards, 4.7 million charge cards and 67.0 million debit cards.

⇨ In 2005, the average number of cards per person was 2.4 credit cards and 1.6 debit cards.

⇨ According to APACS (Association of Payment Clearing Services) in 2005 the volume of online card payments had increased five-fold over the last five years, reaching 310 million for a total of £22.0 billion and accounts for 5% of all personal card payments. 282 plastic transactions took place every second in the UK in 2005.

⇨ There are more credit cards in the UK than people according to APACS. At the end of 2004 there were 74.3m credit and charge cards in the UK compared with around 59 million people in the country.

Servicing debt

⇨ 14 million adults (35%) are relying on their overdrafts to get by each month; 3.5m are permanently overdrawn, while two million workers start the month in their overdraft, even after they have been paid.

⇨ Two million households are living on a financial knife-edge, susceptible to an economic downturn or changes in personal circumstances, according to a recent Financial Services Authority (FSA) report. A further half-million households are already in serious financial difficulty paying bills and meeting debts, the report found.

⇨ The average debt of a client coming to Consumer Credit Counselling Service (CCCS) for advice is now £32,000. The number of people earning more than £30,000 a year who are asking them for help has risen by 257% in the past three years.

⇨ According to a report commissioned by One Advice, nearly 2 million people in the UK have unsecured debts in excess of £10,000. About half a million have unsecured debt higher than £20,000. People in the lower middle-aged bracket (35 to 44-year-olds) were the most likely to have substantial debts that weren't secured, with some 50,000 individuals in that demographic owing more than £10,000.

Students / Youth

⇨ Young people have the highest level of unsecured debt in the UK, with the average person under 30 owing nearly £8,000, recent figures have revealed. People aged between 18 and 29 owe about £7,718 each through credit cards, overdrafts and loans, the equivalent of 36 percent of their total household income, according to Alliance & Leicester. Student loans were found to make up 46% of this figure.

There are more credit cards in the UK than people

⇨ The National Union of Students puts the cost of university, including tuition fees and living expenses, at an estimated £8,810 a year, and more than £10,000 in London.

⇨ A recent FSA survey highlighted:

↳ 29% of 16-24-year-olds said they would not know how to prepare and manage a weekly budget

↳ 19% of 22-24-year-olds have short-term debts over £5,000

↳ 62% of young people said if they got into money trouble or debt they would not be able to name any advice or support services they could turn to for advice

↳ One in five students dropped out of courses; of undergraduates who considered dropping out financial difficulty was a strong factor for 34.4%

↳ 94% of 16-year-olds believe it is important to know how to manage money; only 53% have been taught how to.

Housing

⇨ According to the Department for Communities and Local Government (DCLG) the average house price in the UK in March 2006 stood at £186,519 (£195,001 in England). UK annual house price inflation rose by 3.3%. Annual house price inflation in London was 4.0%.

The majority of people in the UK are not planning ahead sufficiently

⇨ The average house price in the UK in March 2006 for first-time buyers now stands at £145,214 which is an annual increase of 4.2%. (Note: the weightings used were changed for the February 2006 figures. This has had a large impact on the reported average house price for first-time buyers.)

⇨ In the UK, the average deposit required by first-time buyers in Q1 2006 was 17% of the purchase price. Based on repayment loans, in the UK, repayments as a percentage of household income for first-time buyers were 21% in Q1 2006.

⇨ The average Band D council tax bill in England in 2005-2006 was £1,214, and the average increase compared to the previous year was 4.1%.

⇨ Gross mortgage lending totalled £25.1 billion in April 2006 – the highest April lending figure on record according to the latest data from the Council of Mortgage Lenders (CML). Lending was 16% higher than in April 2005 and marks six months of record lending figures.

Major expenses

⇨ The cost of running the average new car has grown to nearly £5,000 a year, or £14 a day, according to the latest RAC Cost of Motoring Index.

⇨ The average wedding costs around £19,595. 45% of couples – some 117,000 nationwide – have no financial planning to pay for the big day, a study by stockbrokers Brewin Dolphin Securities found.

⇨ Parents typically spend £165,668 on raising a child from birth to the age of 21, according to friendly society Liverpool Victoria's most recent annual Cost of a Child survey. This works out at £7,889 a year and represents a rise of 7.8 per cent on last year's survey, more than three times the rate of inflation, and up 18 per cent on the 2003 survey.

Savings

⇨ The majority of people in the UK are not planning ahead sufficiently, and are likely to be storing up problems for the future. 39% of people say they tend to live for today and let tomorrow take care of itself. In the last three years, 28% of people have experienced a large unexpected drop in income, and 21% have faced a large unexpected expense. 70% have made no personal provision to face a drop in income, and 55% do not think they have sufficient provision to face an unexpected expense.

⇨ Half the population (52%) could survive financially for just 17 days, should they suffer an unexpected loss of income, according to research by Combined Insurance.

⇨ FSA research shows that 81% of the pre-retired think that a state pension will not provide them with the standard of living they hope for in retirement. Nevertheless, 37% of these people have not made any additional pension provision.

⇨ According to the latest quarterly National Savings and Investment survey almost half of Brits (45%) do not save regularly.

⇨ Prepared by Credit Action [www.creditaction.org.uk] for the money education website www.moneybasics.co.uk

© Credit Action

Debt advice

Some dos and don'ts

⇨ DO be realistic – face up to your true situation and resolve to deal with it – using the help available to you.

⇨ DO get in touch with your creditors immediately to explain your difficulties.

⇨ DO give priority to those debts which may result in you losing your home, fuel supplies or your liberty.

⇨ DO remember that your creditors prefer small payments regularly rather than larger, irregular payments that you cannot sustain.

⇨ DO reply to creditors' letters and court summonses within the time period specified and let them have all the facts.

⇨ DO keep copies of all correspondence, financial statements, debt schedules etc.

⇨ DO attend and/or be represented at court hearings and take all relevant correspondence with you, including your current financial statement.

⇨ DON'T ignore the problem – it won't go away.

⇨ DON'T give up trying to reach agreement with your creditors even if they are difficult and refuse your initial offers.

⇨ DON'T be threatened or bullied into making promises which you cannot fulfil.

⇨ DON'T borrow more money to pay off your debts, especially by taking on more credit or store cards.

⇨ DON'T be afraid to ask for specialist advice – it's FREE call the Consumer Credit Counselling Service on 0800 1381111

⇨ The above information is reprinted with kind permission from Credit Action. Visit www.creditaction.org.uk for more information.

© Credit Action

Scambuster

Your guide to beating the scammers

Introduction

A scam is a scheme designed to con you out of your cash.

There's a scam out there for everyone. If you let down your guard and think that you won't be fooled, then you too could become a victim.

Scammers are becoming more sophisticated and aim to con us all. Bogus sweepstakes and lotteries, get-rich-quick schemes and fake health cures are some of the favoured means of separating the unwary from their money. But the number of scams just keeps on growing.

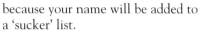

Photo: Pierre-Andre Vullioud

If you think you have been the victim of a scam, or suspect a scam, see the 'What to do if you discover a scam'. No matter how small the amount of money you have lost. It is important that the scamsters are stopped.

Read on to find out how to protect yourself.

Letters predicting the future

What it is

These are one of the most common direct mail scams. Letters from so-called psychics or clairvoyants promise to make predictions that will change the course of your life for ever – for a small fee. Sometimes these mailings are aggressive in tone, saying something bad will happen to you if you do not send them money.

If you send money you are likely to be bombarded with further scams, because your name will be added to a 'sucker' list.

Most likely approach – letter

How to protect yourself

⇨ Stop junk mail by registering with the Mailing Preference Service, so that you can spot scams more easily.

⇨ Don't be intimidated into replying.

Pyramid selling and free gift schemes

What it is

A 'pyramid' scheme is a money-making club which promises, once you've paid a joining fee, that you can earn large amounts by recruiting new members. However, only those at the top make money and the schemes can collapse leaving you out of pocket.

'Matrix' schemes offer a hi-tech gift, like an MP3 player, free. First you have to buy something low value like a mobile telephone signal booster. If you do, you join a waiting list. The person at the top gets their free gift only if a large number of new members signs up – sometimes as many as 100. In reality, most people never get the gift.

Most likely approach – web advert or maybe even a personal approach – from a friend who has been taken in.

How to protect yourself

⇨ Stop, think and be sceptical. Are you being offered something for nothing? If so, why?

⇨ Avoid schemes that offer money based solely on signing up new members.

Lotteries, sweepstakes and competitions

What it is

Every day, people open their post, turn on their computers or switch on their mobile phones to be told they have won something exciting in a prize draw, sweepstake or lottery – without even having entered. While some of these approaches are legitimate, many are dishonest.

You are asked to send an administration fee, but once you've sent your money you may hear nothing more. Or you are told to ring a premium rate 090 number to claim your prize. The longer you stay on the line, the more money the scammer earns. Usually you get nothing in return, but if you do receive something it is worth very little and not what you were promised.

Most likely approach – email, letter, telephone call, text message.

How to protect yourself

⇨ Don't dial an 090 number unless you are absolutely sure how much you will be charged and you are willing to pay for it.

⇨ Remember that if you win something you shouldn't have to pay anything to receive your prize, not even the cost of a telephone call.

Foreign money offers and advance fee scams

What it is

In a letter or email you might be offered a huge sum of money in return for your help to get money out of a foreign country. The scammers use the information you give them to empty your bank account, or to convince you to send them money upfront.

Ads offering you fast loans regardless of your credit history can be another type of advance fee fraud. If you reply, you may be told your loan has been agreed, but before the money can be released you must pay a fee to cover insurance. Once you have paid, you may never hear from the company again.

Most likely approach – letter, email, fax, newspaper ads.

How to protect yourself

⇨ Stop, think and be sceptical. Why

does somebody you don't know want you to send them money upfront? Why should you trust them?

⇨ Never, ever, give your bank details to people you don't know.

Work-from-home opportunities
What it is
These scammers advertise in local newspapers, on lamp posts or on the web. They advertise paid work from home, some making exaggerated claims about potential earnings. But they require money upfront to pay for materials or to reveal their secret. They take your money but some don't pay you for any work you do.

If you do reply to an ad and you're asked for money before you start work, it is likely to be a scam. Genuine employers will not ask for money in advance.

Scammers and fraudsters advertise for people to handle payments on their behalf for a percentage of the money – usually around 10 per cent. You are given a forged or stolen cheque to pay into your account. You are then asked to withdraw the cash to send it to the fraudster by money transfer less your 10 per cent. When the bank finds out the cheque is invalid, they debit your account leaving you out of pocket.
Most likely approach – classified ads, emails.
How to protect yourself
⇨ Stop, think and be sceptical if you are asked for money in advance.
⇨ If you are looking for work to do at home, think about approaching local companies. For more information on homeworking, call the National Group on Homeworking – 0800 174 095, for free advice and information.

Online dating – a dream partner from overseas
What it is
You sign up to an online dating agency and meet someone who is also looking for love. You write to each other for a few months until the person, who happens to live overseas, decides that they want to come to the UK. But they need help with money for the flight. You pay up to help your new friend – but he or she disappears, along with your cash.
Most likely approach – through a website or email.

There's a scam out there for everyone. If you let down your guard and think that you won't be fooled, then you too could become a victim

---

How to protect yourself
⇨ Never send money to someone you don't know, however plausible they sound.
⇨ Report it to the dating site that arranged the introduction.

Golden investment opportunities
What it is
The scamsters will offer you the opportunity to put money into things like shares, fine wine, gemstones, or other 'rare' high value items. The promise is that these will rocket in value.

But what they offer is often over-priced, very high risk and difficult to sell on.

Many scamsters of this type work from overseas. Those dealing with 'investment' may not be authorised by the UK's Financial Services Authority. Therefore you may not get your money back if things go wrong.
Most likely approach – phone, websites.
How to protect yourself
⇨ Stop, think and be sceptical. It is generally against the law in the UK to call people out of the blue to sell them shares.
⇨ Ask for advice. Call the Financial Services Authority on 0845 606 1234 to check whether the company is authorised.
⇨ Get independent financial advice before making an investment.

Miracle health cures
What it is
Pamphlets or advertisements from unscrupulous sellers of medical products often promise 'miracles'. Beware exaggerated claims such as 'instant cures for arthritis', 'lose weight without effort' or 'grow hair overnight'. Similarly, beware of claims that medical appliances, such as hearing aids, are only available from one place.
Most likely approach – advertisement, letter, website.
How to protect yourself
⇨ Stop, think and be sceptical. If something sounds too good to be true it probably is.
⇨ Consult your doctor or pharmacist before you buy any medicinal product by mail order or over the web.

Phishing for your identity
What it is
Phishers send an email or pop-up message that claims to be from an organisation that you may deal with – for example, a bank or auction site. The message may ask you to 'update', 'validate', or 'confirm' your account information. Some phishing emails threaten that there will be consequences if you don't reply.

The messages direct you to a website that looks just like the real thing, but it is in fact a very convincing copy of a genuine site. The sole purpose of the bogus site is to trick you into revealing your personal information and confidential passwords, so the operators can steal your identity and run up bills or commit crimes in your name.

Most likely approach – email.
How to protect yourself
⇨ Stop, think and be sceptical. If you get an email or pop-up message that asks for personal or financial information, do not reply. Don't click on the link in the message either. Legitimate companies don't ask for this type of information by email.
⇨ Check through your credit card and bank statements as soon as you get them for any purchases you don't remember.

What to do if you are unsure about or don't want:
a mailing
⇨ Check if the mailing comes from a member of the Direct Marketing Association (DMA). Go to www.dma.org.uk

⇨ To reduce unwanted mail register, free, with the Mailing Preference Service (go to www.mpsonline.org.uk or call 0845 703 4599). Registering will make it easier for you to spot a scam in your mail.
⇨ If in doubt, bin the letter.
a telephone call
⇨ Telephone Preference Service (TPS): to reduce unwanted sales calls register your telephone number, free, with the TPS – go to www.tpsonline.org.uk or call 0845 070 0707.
⇨ Number block service: many telephone companies offer this service. It blocks callers from the UK and Channel Islands who withhold their number.
⇨ Call barring: you can bar all calls to premium rate services and/or international rate numbers. Some phone companies charge for this service.
⇨ If in doubt, hang up.
a text message
⇨ You cannot be charged for receiving a text unless you sign up to a service.
⇨ If you are signed up to a text message service you don't want, text the word STOP – and the service has to end immediately.

⇨ To reduce unwanted sales text messages register your details with the TPS (see above).
⇨ If in doubt, don't reply.
an email
⇨ Use anti-virus software and a firewall. Keep them up to date.
⇨ Don't email personal or financial information.
⇨ Be cautious opening any attachment or downloading any files from emails you receive, regardless of sender. These files can contain viruses or other software that can weaken your computer's security.
⇨ If in doubt, don't reply.

What to do if you discover a scam
Tell your friends and family. If you think you have been the victim of a scam, or you suspect a scam, call Consumer Direct for clear, practical consumer advice 08454 04 05 06 www.consumerdirect.gov.uk

⇨ The above information is reprinted with kind permission from Consumer Direct. Visit wwwconsumerdirect.gov.uk for more.
© Crown copyright

Scammers create web of deceit

With online scamming on the increase top psychologist Donna Dawson explains why consumers are still too trusting online

Trusting UK consumers are not prepared enough for the potential scams that exist online, an ICM[1] survey by Get Safe Online has found, despite the fact that two-thirds (66%) – approximately 19 million people – have been confronted with a suspicious email or website, and over one-third (39%) – around 11 million people – have received spurious emails asking for banking details or advising them of a lottery win or inheritance.

Increasingly, scammers are creating emails which are so convincing that they appear to be from legitimate companies, by using corporate logos

with links to highly sophisticated fake websites. Despite this, online shoppers and surfers are still not taking adequate precautions to protect themselves online, and this has led to concerns that UK consumers are too trusting and likely to believe a tempting email offer.

In the survey of men and women aged over 18 years around 8 million (29%) are not aware, or aware but unsure of protective measures, that fraudsters now have the ability to copy real websites and lure people to a fraudulent website with an attractive and realistic-looking email offer. By considering replying to these kinds

of emails, consumers are putting themselves at risk of having their money stolen by a fraudster.

Two-thirds (66%) – approximately 19 million people – have been confronted with a suspicious email or website

In addition, the survey found that almost half (45%), around 17 million people, would not automatically delete an unusual or unfamiliar email, despite the increase in scamming online and a recorded 5.7 billion phishing emails sent each month (Anti-Phishing Working Group figures) – that's almost one for every person in the planet. Over a quarter (28%) of people felt that reading the email carefully and trusting their instincts is an acceptable measure to avoid being a victim of online fraud, and 24% felt that simply asking a friend for advice would be sufficient.

'Consumers are still treading in unfamiliar territory when it comes to recognising scams online; most online users are not that technically sophisticated'

Donna Dawson, psychologist, commented: 'Consumers are still treading in unfamiliar territory when it comes to recognising scams online; most online users are not that technically sophisticated, and so are usually unaware of what to look out for. Even when they are aware to some degree, the computer screen offers a false sense of security: not having the scamming person in front of you, either vocally or physically, gives the consumer time to think things over, providing the illusion that he/she has arrived at a carefully-thought-through, or instinctive, conclusion. However, a decision made without all the facts, or one made on "gut instinct" alone, is no substitute for knowledge.'

Nick Staib from Get Safe Online said: 'It is important that consumers are aware of the increase and professionalism of online scammers. You wouldn't let a suspicious sales person into your house; and the same amount of caution should be taken when receiving emails from unfamiliar people or companies.

'Conmen prey on trusting consumers and there are a number of protective measures that people can take. We urge people to seek advice from an experienced source and visit the Get Safe Online website if they are unsure about anything they receive.'

Authoritative and impartial free advice on how to protect yourself from fraudsters can be found at www. getsafeonline.org

The key points are as follows:

⇨ Never give out personal financial details via email.
⇨ Trust your more paranoid instincts. If you think someone is trying to con you, stand back from the situation and take stock. Buy yourself some time if you can; for example take a number and promise to call back.
⇨ Shred personal documents before throwing them out.
⇨ Be conscious of what is personal information: bank details, credit card numbers, passwords are obvious but a fraudster can make use of trivial information such as where you work, information about friends and family etc.
⇨ Be careful what you publish about yourself online.
⇨ Check credentials carefully. For example, if someone claims to be working for a lottery company, look up the number on Yell.com or BT.com and call them and check.
⇨ Be firm. Conmen can be very persistent and persuasive; playing

on human emotions like guilt, greed and the desire to be liked. Stick to your guns.
⇨ Discuss the problem and set ground rules for family members and, in a business environment, for colleagues.

For all the information you need visit www.getsafeonline.org
[1] ICM interviewed a random sample of 627 adults with Internet access aged 18+ by telephone across the country between 24th-25th May 2006. ICM is a member of the British Polling Council and abides by its rules. Further information at: www.icmresearch. co.uk.
20 June 2006

⇨ The above information is re-printed with kind permission from Get Safe Online. Visit www.getsafeonline.org for more information.

Absolutely ethical, darling!

As the world's biggest organic food store is set to open in Britain, eco-friendly holidays soar and Ford invests £1bn in greener cars, Adam Edwards says we've all gone ethical

Thirty-five years ago, the first ethical handbook for hippies was published. *Alternative London* was a slim volume that advised the 'children of the revolution' on everything important to them, from squatting to sex to LSD trips.

Among its 200 pages of 'right-on' information (which included tips on hitchhiking to Dover and where to buy the cheapest cork wall tiles), it devoted half a chapter to what it described as 'the brown is beautiful cult for food that must be produced without artificial means'.

Unfortunately, the book could only unearth half-a-dozen health-food shops, dusty emporiums that smelled of camphor and sold Horlicks and *Health & Efficiency* magazine, but where one could purchase at least some of the recommended brown rice and lentils. There was only one shop entirely dedicated to a hippie's nutrient needs. It was at 113 Baker Street in London and called itself Wholefood.

How far have we come! This autumn, the biggest organic shop on the planet will be launched in Britain. In what was once London's grandest department store, Barkers, an enormous superstore is to be opened by the world's biggest and most profitable organic grocer, the American supermarket chain called, incidentally, Whole Foods.

Three-and-a-half decades after the sandal-clad pilgrims trudged up Baker Street to what is now, ironically, a Nando's chicken restaurant, Britain's environmentally concerned consumer is the driving force behind a £25 billion-a-year business, of which £4 billion comes from food and drink sales.

The jokes about knitting one's own yogurt and tree-hugging are as dated as big shoulder pads and hard hair. 'Ethical consumerism', as it is called, is now mainstream and most major companies – and David Cameron – have realised the need to ride its wave.

> ## 'Ethical consumerism', as it is called, is now mainstream and most major companies have realised the need to ride its wave

Marks & Spencer's very public preoccupation with fair trade, compassionate farming and bio-degradable sandwich wrappers are just as much a feature of its high-street revival as its fashion campaign featuring Twiggy and assorted supermodels.

'Even companies such as Tesco are finally having to join in with ethical consumerism because they don't want to be seen in a bad light,' says Ruth Russelson of *Ethical Consumer* magazine.

This week, the Ford Motor Company announced it is dropping its research on developing faster and more powerful 'boy racers' to concentrate on environmentally safer cars. It is to plough at least £1 billion into developing greener cars in Britain over the next six years, developing lightweight materials, advanced diesel and petrol engines, hybrids and biofuels.

'Environmental motoring has to go mainstream, it cannot just be a lifestyle choice of the concerned,' said Lewis Booth, Ford's executive vice-president.

Ford's announcement coincides with BP's advertising campaign promoting its investments in solar and wind power as 'Beyond petroleum', while the cut-price clothing retailer Primark has unveiled plans to join the Ethical Trading Initiative (an alliance of retailers and unions that promotes respect for the rights of poor workers in factories and farms worldwide).

Photo: Chris Chidsey

While conspicuous consumption of airline fuel, among other unethical indulgences, has barely troubled holidaymakers in the past, it was reported this week that there has been a surge in ethical travel.

'Our bookings are double what they were this time last year,' says Justin Francis, the managing director of Responsible Travel. 'Tourism is one of the world's biggest industries and yet until the last three years it has been untouched by a strong ethical dimension. We are belatedly catching up.'

It was not too long ago that ethical consumerism – it sounds less sexy than a bowl of muesli – was believed to be the preserve of worthy, joyless cranks.

Nobody would dream of photographing WAGs on a retail therapy jag for fair trade goods. There was no glamour in boycotting a foreign sweatshop or gossiping about energy-efficient light bulbs. Only the Prince of Wales appeared to be keeping the subject in the public domain and he seemed to be ploughing a lonely furrow.

But the truth is that this dull public image of shopping with a conscience has been at odds with many British consumers, who have, without fuss, been insisting on buying products that are not harmful to the environment and society. The reasons for this increasing ethical purchasing have been threefold.

First, it is only in the past two or three years that global warming has, for many, become a reality rather than scaremongering or scientific mumbo-jumbo.

Now that respected figures such as the naturalist Sir David Attenborough have announced that they are no longer sceptical about climate change, the public have started to make a positive contribution to containing global warming by thinking about how and what they consume.

Second, the disillusionment with modern politics, spin and sleaze has left many of us feeling impotent. Buying ethically is one way of taking the power back into our hands and feeling good about what we are doing.

Finally, ethical consumer goods can now be found everywhere. Only a few years ago, one had to trawl the most obscure places to find an ethical brand. Nowadays, the fair trade and organic symbols are universal and readily available ethical brands are taking us from birth to death.

Fair trade food and drink sales increased by 52 per cent in 2005. Waitrose reported an increase last year of 20 per cent in its organic lines, and fresh food from regional suppliers was up by 60 per cent. The Soil Association, the organic farming body, claims sales of organic food, particularly baby food, increased by nearly a third in 2005.

According to the Institute for Grocery Distribution, shoppers are increasingly prepared to pay a premium for organic, free-range or fair trade products. It concludes that the ethical trend is growing so fast that soon it will apply as much to toothpaste, soap, tea towels and clothes as it does to organic milk, free-range eggs and fair trade coffee.

Indeed, environmentally friendly and cruelty-free detergents and cosmetics are as effective – and packaged just as attractively – as their more toxic counterparts. It is now possible to buy fair trade jeans on the high street, while the exclusive Enamore label is selling organic lingerie ('French Knickers' and 'Bralettes') made from hemp.

It was not too long ago that ethical consumerism – it sounds less sexy than a bowl of muesli – was believed to be the preserve of worthy, joyless cranks

---

And it is not just about how you live, but how you die, too. Funerals designed to have a minimum impact on the environment, with bodies buried in biodegradable caskets made of paper, willow or bamboo, are the fastest-growing trend in the burial market.

'The rate of growth in natural burial is infinitely faster than the rate of growth in crematoria 100 years ago,' says Mike Jarvis of the Natural Death Centre.

I would argue that the tipping point for the surge in ethical consumerism, when it moved from the hippie-dippy fringe into the mainstream, was the introduction of GM crops in the late 1990s.

The outcry over the introduction of engineered food was not just from radical groups, but from organisations as weighty as the Women's Institute and the Welsh Assembly.

These concerns fed into the legacy of mad-cow disease and other assorted food scares of the 1980s and 1990s, which had made us reassess the quality of what we eat and drink.

So, moral consumer power is changing the way our major companies do business – and they are reaping the profits as a result. Now, the imminent arrival of Whole Foods looks set to turn ethical consumerism into a mass-market movement. Its success in America has forced Wal-Mart, the world's biggest retailer, to start promoting organic foods.

The Whole Foods founder, John Mackey, describes his company as a 'virtuous circle entwining the food chain, human beings and the earth; each reliant upon the others through a delicate symbiosis'.

Rather less pompously he says: 'When we started 25 years ago, we were very much on the fringe. It has only been in the past few years that we have moved into the mainstream. We have not really changed. What has changed is that the world has begun to move closer to us.'

Or, to put it another way, Britain, which has led the world in ethical consumerism and is the reason for Mackey siting the world's biggest organic store here, is now prepared to put its money where its campaigning mouth has been for decades.
19 July 2006

Ethical consumerism

Co-op bank warns against complacency as ethical sales and boycotts outstrip beer and fags sales

The value of UK ethical consumerism last year exceeded the sales of 'over-the-counter' beer and cigarettes, according to the Co-operative Bank's annual *Ethical Consumerism Report* published today (27 November).

The Report, which acts as a barometer of ethical spending in the UK, shows that in 2005 UK ethical consumerism was worth £29.3 billion, for the first time overtaking the retail market for tobacco and alcohol which stood at £28.0 billion.

Ethical consumerism in 2005 was up 11 per cent on the previous year. Over the same period, UK household expenditure increased by only 1.4 per cent

---

However, the Co-operative Bank was quick to guard against complacency and cautioned against interpreting this growth as a sign that the markets were capable of delivering sustainable solutions without intervention.

The Report, which is published in conjunction with The Future Foundation, shows that ethical consumerism in 2005 was up 11 per cent on the previous year. Over the same period, UK household expenditure increased by only 1.4 per cent.

Spending on ethical food which includes organic products, Fairtrade goods and free-range eggs was up 18 per cent from £4.6 billion to £5.4 billion. Green home expenditure, which incorporates energy-efficient electrical appliances, green mortgage repayments, small renewables (such as micro-wind turbines) and green energy, was up from £3.8 billion to £4.1 billion.

Eco-travel and transport costs, which includes environmentally friendly transport, responsible tour operators, public transport and sales of green cars, was up from £1.7 billion to £1.8 billion.

Spending on personal products, such as humane cosmetics and eco-fashion, was up five per cent to £1.3 billion. Monies in ethical finance, which includes ethical banking and investments, stood at £11.6 billion, up from £10.6 billion last year.

Executive Director of Business Management Craig Shannon said: 'The fact that the value of ethical consumerism is now higher than the retail figures for cigarettes and beers is a milestone. However, total ethical spending is spread over a wide range of products and services, and in very few markets has it become the market norm. Overall, spend on ethical foods still only accounts for five per cent of the typical shopping basket.

'Where the ethical or eco-choice has become the market leader, for example in sales of A-rated energy fridges (which account for some 60 per cent of the market), this has been underpinned by an EU labelling scheme, inefficient products being removed from sale and the support of well-targeted subsidies.

'If, as many scientists are saying, we have ten years to make a dent in climate change, it is this type of radical overhaul of the choices made available to people that is going to deliver the rapid market changes required.

'The efforts of far-sighted, highly motivated consumers need to be leveraged and supported with business innovation and government intervention.'
27 November 2006

⇨ The above information is reprinted with kind permission from the Co-operative Bank. Visit www.co-operativebank.co.uk for more information.

© Co-operative Bank

What assures consumers?

An AccountAbility/National Consumer Council Report – executive summary

Consumers consistently say they are concerned about the impact of the products they purchase, and that they prefer to buy from companies that take social and environmental responsibilities seriously. But there remains a major gap between consumers' concern and everyday action – even where basic information to guide choices is readily available. For example, nearly 90% of people in the UK say they oppose caged egg production, but only 50% of eggs sold by major supermarkets are free range; more than 80% of shoppers want to reduce food miles, but only a quarter look at country of origin labels; and over a quarter of people say they would pay a little more for a green electricity tariff, but only a very small minority have actually made the switch.

> **Nearly 90% of people in the UK say they oppose caged egg production, but only 50% of eggs sold by major supermarkets are free range**

If this is not just a sign of wishful thinking and self-delusion by both consumers and pollsters, it is a serious missed opportunity to help align markets towards sustainability. While consumers are not the only stakeholders concerned with corporate responsibility (CR), they can be a critical driver of change. Conversely there is a real risk that the progress towards more sustainable businesses and markets will be undermined in the longer term if consumers are not engaged. There are a number of theories about the causes of the persistent gap between consumers expressed concerns and their actual purchasing choices:

By Maya Forstater and Jeannette Oelschaegel with Maria Sillanpää

⇨ The myth of the ethical consumer. Consumers in general are only paying lip service to CR issues and are more concerned about things like price, quality, convenience and status.

⇨ Too much information, too little time. Consumers just do not have the time to evaluate all the information available to them and are put off by the complexity and disputed nature of many sustainability issues.

⇨ I will if you will. It is not lack of information that prevents consumers acting but habits and cultural norms; role models and word-of-mouth communication has not been fully utilised to overcome consumer inertia and scepticism.

⇨ Organisational disconnect. Organisations' CR strategies are simply detached from consumers' interests and expectations and are not communicated well at brand and product levels.

⇨ Dysfunctional relations. Public debate about sustainability issues remains dominated by one-sided arguments, scaremongering, spin and incomprehensible jargon from all sides: consumers do not know whom to trust.

These theories are not mutually exclusive; in fact they are all useful in explaining the gap between consumer concerns and action. In the past two decades attention has turned to using insights into consumer behaviour to develop tools and strategies to align business behaviour and consumer concerns.

Two broad waves of approaches have been seen:

⇨ Information was the focus of the 1st wave of approaches in the 1980s and 1990s. Ethical consumer guides, boycott campaigns and the promotion of certification and labelling schemes such as Fairtrade, Forest Stewardship Council and organic food aimed to raise awareness and provide information about the impacts of different products and companies.

⇨ Motivation is the focus of the 2nd wave, where in the last few years companies have more explicitly explored how they can build brand reputation by aligning with consumers' concerns and desires. This approach recognises that customers do not necessarily want to 'read the small print' underlying their purchasing choices but that they do expect companies that they trust to act in a trustworthy manner.

Businesses are now recognising that social and environmental concerns are becoming mainstream and that is a licence for businesses who share those same concerns to engage with their customers and find new ways to turn this into business value. In order for any approach to aligning mainstream brands with consumers' values to succeed in impacting on consumer choices it must not just concentrate on the positive drivers of consumer behaviour, but also on what holds people back. Human beings are not actually all that good at things like

Photo: Marco Michelini

judging accuracy, thinking about long-term risk and maximising their own utility. What they are very good at is sniffing out hypocrisy, bad motives and lies. These are the skills that consumers use to guide their choices in the marketplace, and it is this scepticism that effective consumer assurance has to address.

Assurance is not about a particular technical methodology or process but about achieving the outcome whereby consumers gain confidence in the information they base their decisions on, and the confidence that these decisions will not backfire on them. It is clear that the majority of consumers do not, and are unlikely to start, considering their ethical positions like a set of technical specifications and then choosing the company or product that best meets these demands. For consumers 'what assures?' is about what underpins the implicit trust they have in a company, product or brand that enables them to choose and keep choosing a company with confidence that it operates fairly and with responsibility.

Consumer confidence can be supported by a combination of formal and informal claims and messages coming from within companies, from outsiders and from partners (such as NGOs, labelling bodies and government agencies). This assurance can be attached to specific products, or more generally to the brand. There is no single route to assuring stakeholders, and all routes are subject to the enormous pressure of distrust. Effective assurance at a company level needs to be based on a joined-up approach which crosses over functions of operational management and partnerships, formal assurance schemes, marketing and corporate communication.

Formal certification, labelling and award schemes can play a key role in consumer assurance, but they do not work alone. Labelling schemes such as Fairtrade and organic farming have had considerable success. They provide sufficient rigour, are backed by trusted organisations and have been picked up by wider movements and opinion leaders. But such labels can add to confusion when there are too many or when their meaning is not clear. Beyond such standardised labelling schemes some companies have sought to develop a bespoke labelling or endorsement relationship with an individual expert, NGO or opinion leader, sometimes stepping into the grey area in the overlap between product endorsement and on-pack campaigning.
July 2006

⇨ The above information is reprinted with kind permission from the National Consumer Council. Please visit the National Consumer Council website at www.ncc.org.uk for more information.

© National Consumer Council

Ethical food

'Green is the new black' as Brits turn to ethical food

Latest research from Mintel finds the move towards buying ethical foods* is more than just a flash in the pan. British shoppers are set to spend over £2 billion on ethical foods this year alone, up by a massive 62% since 2002. People in Britain today are clearly moving towards more ethical lifestyles and are starting to realise that their actions all have consequences. As British shoppers increasingly look to shop with a clear conscience, Mintel forecasts that the market will continue to grow for the foreseeable future.

In a country once dominated by a throwaway culture, three-quarters (75%) of British now believe that people have a duty to recycle, up from 65% in 2002. Similarly, a third (34%) 'buy Fairtrade where available', up from just one in four (26%) in 2002 and two in five (40%) now 'buy free-range products whenever they can' (up from 33% in 2002). Where once price was all important, rising disposable income and a generally more affluent society has allowed people to start living up to their ethics and a third of adults now believe it is worth paying more for Fairtrade, organic and locally sourced foods.

People in Britain today are clearly moving towards more ethical lifestyles and are starting to realise that their actions all have consequences

---

'Ethical-food suppliers have traded on the fringes of the UK grocery market for many years and until recently only a few sectors, such as free-range eggs, had really established themselves. But now many more ethical products have entered the mainstream-foods sector, with leading suppliers and retailers becoming increasingly involved. In the present climate, many companies may be hoping to improve their profile by projecting a more ethical stance. But whatever their reasonings for choosing the ethical route, this movement is certainly a step in the right direction towards a more ethically-minded society. With these products becoming rapidly more widely available, the market is set to see substantial future growth,' comments Julie Sloan, senior market analyst at Mintel.

According to the Mintel Global New Products Database, there were some 70 ethical food products launched last year in the UK alone, up from just 25 in 2002. So far this year, the Mintel GNPD has recorded 53 new ethical food launches, with the beverages sector proving to be the most prolific producers of ethical new products.

Fairtrade is king of the crop
Within the ethical foods market, Fairtrade is the real star performer in terms of sales growth. Fairtrade is

set to be worth £230 million by the end of this year, experiencing some 265% growth between 2002 and 2006 alone. What is more, Mintel predicts that Fairtrade will see a further 138% growth over the next five years, with sales crashing through the half a billion pound mark (£547 million) by 2011.

Barbara Crowther from the Fairtrade Foundation says: 'Mintel's latest insights confirm what the Fairtrade Foundation is experiencing on a daily basis – rapidly growing consumer and business interest in Fairtrade and wider ethical food shopping. This shows no signs of abating, and is also moving beyond the food sector for us now. The challenge now is to consolidate long-term Fairtrade commitments as part of mainstream consumer and business behaviour, in order to bring about tangible and sustainable change for millions more producers in developing countries.'

The buck stops here

While almost three in five adults (56%) believe that 'we are all responsible for what we choose to buy', many feel that the government, manufacturers and supermarkets should also shoulder at least some of the responsibility to buy ethically. Today, one in four (25%) adults believe it is down to the manufacturers to be more ethical, while a substantial number say it is the government's (28%) or the supermarkets' (24%) responsibility to introduce regulations.

* includes organic food, Fairtrade mark (clothes, food and other products), farmers markets, free-range eggs and freedom food

About Mintel

Mintel is a worldwide leader of competitive media, product and consumer intelligence. For more than 35 years, Mintel has provided key insight into leading global trends. With offices in Chicago, London, Belfast and Sydney, Mintel's innovative product line provides unique data that has a direct impact on client success. For more information on Mintel, please visit their website at www.mintel.com. *August 2006*

⇨ The above information is reprinted with kind permission from Mintel. Visit www.mintel.com

© Mintel

Photo: Meliha Gojak

Fair trade

With the explosion of fair trade products in high street shops, supermarkets and online stores, you can ensure that the money you spend makes a real difference to the lives of the people who make your goods

What is fair trade?

In simple terms, fair trade is about improving the income that goes to the farm workers at the beginning of a supply chain. You might be shocked

---

Fair trade is about improving the income that goes to the farm workers at the beginning of a supply chain

---

to learn how little of the £2.50 that you pay for your tall, ultra-skinny, frothy mocha cappuccino goes to the farmer in Costa Rica who harvested the coffee beans that made it. What's worse is that many of the commodities that poor people across the developing world depend on to make a living – such as coffee, cocoa or cotton – are vulnerable to sharp drops in their global price. A fall in the price of a product like coffee by even just a few pence can put a family in the developing world out of business, which would mean that they'd be unable to pay for food, water, shelter, health care, education and much more.

Fair trade products seek to address this vulnerability by paying poor producers more than they'd normally receive. This 'premium' provides them with greater economic support when world prices fluctuate, as well as extra funds for investment in land, shelter, education and health care.

Fair trade products seek to address this vulnerability by paying poor producers more than they'd normally receive. This 'premium' provides them with greater economic support when world prices fluctuate, as well as extra funds for investment in land, shelter, education and health care.

The Fairtrade mark

The Fairtrade Foundation was established in 1992 by CAFOD, Christian Aid, New Consumer, Oxfam, Traidcraft and the World Development Movement (and later joined by the Women's Institute). Its Fairtrade mark is placed on products that have met their strict standards in order to offer a fair deal for farmers in developing countries. These standards ensure that:
⇨ Farmers receive a fair and stable price for their products;
⇨ Farmers and plantation workers have the opportunity to improve their lives;
⇨ Producers have greater respect for the environment;
⇨ Small-scale farmers gain a stronger position in world markets;
⇨ A closer link is formed between consumers and producers.

Fair and ethical trade

In strict definitions, fair trade is different to ethical trade. Ethical trade is about improving the conditions in which goods are produced. For example, ethical trade can ensure that workers are able to join a union, have contracts for their jobs, work reasonable hours in safe conditions, and get adequate breaks and holidays. High-profile campaigns against the 'sweatshop' conditions of factories in Asia belonging to global corporate giants have raised public awareness about the need for ethical trading standards.

The Ethical Trading Initiative (ETI) is a partnership of high street companies, non-governmental organisations (NGOs) and trade unions, with support from the government. The ETI's aim is to ensure that internationally recognised labour standards, including human rights in the workplace, are observed at all stages in the production of high street goods sold in the UK.

Although fair trade and ethical trade are based on different principles, they go hand-in-hand for those who want to shop with a conscience, since both aim to benefit the lives of workers in some of the world's poorest countries.

Buying fair trade products

The future looks bright for fair trade sales in the UK, where recognition of the Fairtrade mark has doubled since 2002. What's more, the British love of coffee, bananas, tea and chocolate has meant that the country is now the biggest market for Fairtrade products in the world.

The Fairtrade logo can be found on over 250 different products sold in high street shops, supermarkets, online stores, cafés and restaurants. To find your nearest fair trade supplier, contact the British Association for Fair Trade Shops

⇨ The above information is reprinted with kind permission from TheSite.org. Visit www.thesite.org for more information.

© TheSite.org

The Fairtrade revolution

How consumer power sparked a Fairtrade revolution on our high streets – businesses show their credentials, with varying levels of success

A trio of cartoon superheroes blazes a trail across the front page of the latest issue of the fair trade and ethical lifestyle magazine, *New Consumer*. But the smiley faces are not those of contented coffee farmers from Colombia or banana workers in the Windward Islands.

They are the more recognisable features of those considered by some campaigners as high street bad guys, such as Sir Terry Leahy, chief executive of Tesco. The picture results from a series of deals between the Fairtrade organisation and big-name businesses which could further propel ethically sourced products from the margins to the mainstream.

It promises to boost the wealth of some farmers in developing countries but has inevitably led some in the west to wonder if supermarkets are exploiting – if not taking over – a valued charitable brand. 'I think it is a very interesting debate but our first and major concern is whether we can increase opportunities for creating wealth for more farmers in developing countries,' said Harriet Lamb, the executive director of Fairtrade, yesterday. 'That is the

By Terry Macalister

beginning and end of everything we do.'

Among the 'groundbreaking' initiatives launched in recent days is the announcement from Marks & Spencer that it will switch all its tea and coffee to Fairtrade-certified produce.

Flowers and footie

Meanwhile Virgin Trains is doing the same and switching to Fairtrade for its hot drinks served on mainline rail services. They join a growing band of more than 200 companies who sell everything from Fairtrade wine, flowers and T-shirts all the way through to footballs.

14 years ago Fairtrade was established as a charity which promised to bring a decent deal to isolated coffee and other agricultural producers in the developing world who were faced with a crash in commodity prices.

Its recent success has been dramatic as western consumers demand more information and higher standards from those they buy from. Sales of Fairtrade products rose 40% in 2005 alone and are now worth £195m annually – tiny by total consumer spending, but part of a growing trend.

And the willingness of the big brands to stock ethical products is expected to lead to further success. 'A study carried out for us showed that the public tends to stick to old habits when they go out shopping,' said Ms Lamb. '36 per cent of those surveyed who knew about Fairtrade cited lack of visibility as the biggest barrier to increasing purchases of Fairtrade products,' she added.

Stuart Rose, the chief executive of M&S and another of *New Consumer*'s superheroes, confirmed he is already looking at stocking even more Fairtrade products. 'We have already received such positive feedback from customers we will be extending the range further this autumn,' he said.

Community benefit

Silver Kasaro-Atwoki from the Mabale Growers' Tea Factory in Uganda is also in no doubt about the importance of Fairtrade – for himself, but also for a much wider group of stakeholders.

'Through Fairtrade we have been able to change our agricultural techniques to improve the quality and quantity of our teas. But we have also opened new access roads which have benefited all in the community.'

There are 1,500 Fairtrade products available from more than 150 companies, but Fairtrade bananas, for example, still only account for about 5% of the total British banana market

---

There is little external sign that Fairtrade has succumbed to all this flattering attention from money-machines such as Tesco. The charity's head office is still based in a non-descript warren of workshops formerly used by jewellers from nearby Hatton Garden, central London. And while Ms Lamb is happy to admit that the organisation's financial fortunes have been transformed, she says the 35 staff – up from 10 in 2001 – are only able to do a tiny fraction of what they would like to.

Of the 8,000 events put on to celebrate the current Fairtrade Fortnight, which runs to March 19, only a handful have been organised by paid staff in London. The rest are down to local volunteers and campaigners.

But would it matter if supermarkets are cynically trying to use Fairtrade to increase their power over their rivals, consumers and suppliers?

'We need to look at the motivation of why companies are doing it but that is a good news story as well,' said Ms Lamb. 'Companies are doing it because their customers want it. And you can argue to what extent it's the role of business to take on the role of sustainable development. I would say it's an essential part of their business. Others might disagree but no one would disagree it's the business of business to do what customers want.'

Three quarters of Fairtrade income comes from the companies who pay for the organisation's certification – now worth £2.6m annually – but Ms Lamb says it will always stick to raising 25% from other sources – be that government or private donations.

But there is conversely a financial problem for some agricultural communities struggling to pay the cost of Fairtrade certification.

Ms Lamb says her organisation is keenly aware of this issue and attempts to conquer it through the provision of its own grants.

No organic guarantee

She is also happy to dispel the notion that Fairtrade is synonymous with organic produce.

'Often the farmers – say living in the Peruvian mountains who obviously care for their local environment – want to go organic but people understand that Fairtrade is different from organic – it's not the same – and there are many farmers who simply can't go organic. For example because they are surrounded by large plantations who spray [pesticides].'

The increasing involvement of supermarkets and other traditional brands is also beginning to dispel the notion that ethical consumers come from a relatively small and affluent group, says Ms Lamb.

'Some people assume that it's a middle-class preoccupation, but that is slightly arrogant I would say. In fact if you look it's often true that people on lower incomes give a higher percentage of income to charity.

'I visited a homeless project where people have coffee shops on the high street in Edinburgh and they are selling 100% Fairtrade coffee because they say "we know what it's like for those farmers and we want to play our part in making a difference".'

It's wrong to imagine that it is only the more affluent who are willing to go out there and put the needs of people in developing countries first, argues Ms Lamb.

'As we see with the incredible success of Fairtrade with the Co-op and Asda it is people across the spectrum who are ready to buy Fairtrade. In fact, awareness of Fairtrade products is growing fastest among social groups C and D.'

FAQ: trade benefits

What is the Fairtrade Foundation?
It is a charity that is based around an independent consumer label promising to ensure a fair financial return for producers in developing countries.

What can consumers expect when buying a Fairtrade product?

To use the mark, companies such as the supermarkets must source from producers that have been inspected and certified according to international Fairtrade standards.

How do the 5 million farmers and workers covered by the scheme benefit?
They are paid a guaranteed price that not only covers the cost of sustainable production and living but also gives a premium to allow them to invest in business development, plus social or environmental projects.

What happens if the price of coffee rises above the Fairtrade price?
The farmers' price moves up along with global commodity prices but never falls below the guaranteed level.

Are ethical products really sweeping the consumer world?
There are 1,500 products available from more than 150 companies, but Fairtrade bananas, for example, still only account for about 5% of the total British banana market.
8 March 2006

Supermarkets vs local shops

To many, supermarkets are an integral part of modern life, but should their expansion be at the cost of local stores? TheSite. org looks at the pros and cons of supermarket shopping

For supermarkets

⇨ Time savers: Let's be honest, life without supermarkets would be total hell. Gone are the days of trawling the high street all day long, and now we can fit shopping into our busy schedules. We're not even restricted by opening hours, with many supermarkets now open 24 hours.

⇨ Choice: Supermarkets now offer the choice of up to 40,000 lines – everything from economy to niche products at competitive prices; they provide free car-parking, home deliveries and internet shopping. And you can get supposed seasonal vegetables all year round.

⇨ Transport links: There are bus schemes; a number of outlets offer taxi services; and some are investigating outlets on estates, although high crime is putting them off.

⇨ Affordable: Supermarkets have reduced the cost of some grocery shopping and made one-time luxuries into basics, which means many of us whose outgoings often exceed their incomings on payday do not starve.

Against supermarkets

⇨ Overkill: Supermarket competitiveness can harm local food economies that sustain our market towns and villages, the food producers who supply them, and the people who depend on them. Their monopoly position in the market allows them to dictate how much they pay farmers, while at the same time seeking out cheaper food from abroad.

⇨ Exclusive: Not all consumers are in easy reach of a supermarket. Hard as it may be to believe, there are those who have no car, no internet, and whose shopping budgets are too small to qualify for home deliveries.

⇨ Unsociable: The glazed expression of a supermarket checkout girl does not offer the social contact and conversation that can be found in a local shop, for some this is the only brush with other people they get each day.

Supermarket competitiveness can harm local food economies that sustain our market towns and villages, the food producers who supply them, and the people who depend on them

---

⇨ Local shops: When superstores open, small shops close. Not always, but it does happen, especially when ridiculously oversized stores open on the local shop's doorstep.

⇨ Freshness: Local markets and shops tend to stock fresher local produce rather than the standardised symmetrical blander vegetables you will find in supermarkets.

Fixing the local/ supermarket divide

The industry has put together a code of practice to monitor the relationship between retailers and suppliers. All supermarkets, where they can, will use local suppliers. But it is paramount that these suppliers comply with appropriate legislation; that the quality of their products is first class and that production is adequate for the stores' needs. The supermarkets have not wiped out the local shops; they just mean that you, the consumer, are not totally dependent on them. If people want to keep their local shops alive and well, shoppers will need to buy more than the odd loaf and a tin of beans from the grocer's at the weekend. Even so, it's likely that many will continue to shop at supermarkets because of the convenience and choice.

⇨ The above information is reprinted with kind permission from TheSite.org. Visit www.thesite.org for more information.

© TheSite.org

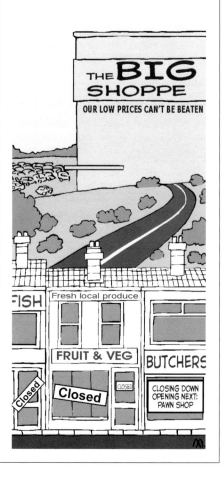

Rise of the supermarkets?

Statistics taken from the Competition Commission's *Groceries Market Investigation.*

Grocery retailing in the UK – number of outlets.

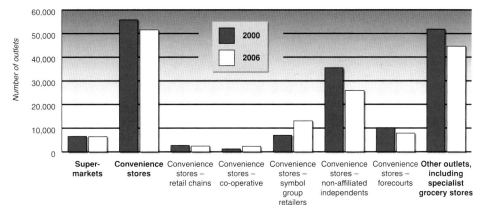

Total outlets in 2000 = 114,162
Total outlets in 2006 = 102,511

Grocery retailing in the UK – sales.

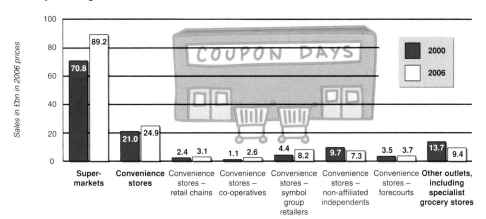

Total sales in 2000 = £105.7bn
Total sales in 2006 = £123.5bn

Notes

1. Figures do not sum due to rounding.
2. In relation to convenience stores: retail chains include, for example, Sainsbury's and Tesco; co-operatives include, for example, The Co-operative Group; symbol group retailers include, for example, Spar and Costcutter; forecourts include, for example, Shell and BP.
3. In relation to other outlets, these include off-licences as well as specialist grocery stores such as butchers and bakers.
4. Excludes joint ventures to avoid double counting store numbers.

Source: CC analysis of data from IGD, UK Grocery Retailing, *2001 and 2006, and IGD,* UK Convenience Retailing, *2006.*

Number of UK stores operated by the UK's largest grocery retailers.

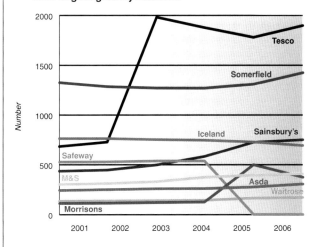

Note: store numbers include both supermarkets and convenience stores.

Source: IGD, Grocery retailing, September 2006.

Specialist grocery stores in the UK.

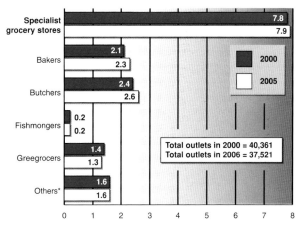

Sales in £bn in 2005 prices

* Includes delicatessens, cheese shops and chocolatiers, but does not include off-licences.

Source: Verdict, Neighbourhood retailing, 2006.

Source: Groceries Market Investigation, the Competition Commission, 23 January 2007

KEY FACTS

⇨ Being a good consumer means knowing what to look out for and what to avoid. It means knowing where and how to get the best value for money, where to go if things go wrong. (page 1)

⇨ Spending has hit a record high as British consumers parted with as much as £1 trillion (a million million) in 2005 alone. On average this works out at around £37,000 for every household across Britain today. (page 3)

⇨ Half of consumers said that, when faced with problems in the last year, they didn't complain because procedures are too long-winded and tiresome. (page 6)

⇨ Advertising today is a major industry. Each year between 1-2% of all income in the UK is spent on advertising. Without advertising, there would be no radio or television, very few magazines and newspapers and no 'free' newspapers. (page 7)

⇨ The impact of the consumer society is now so deep that seven out of 10 three-year-olds recognise the McDonald's logo but only half know their own surname, said a left-of-centre think-tank. (page 11)

⇨ The child-orientated market in the UK is now worth £30 billion. (page 12)

⇨ Previous studies have suggested 90% of shopaholics are women, but in the latest study psychologists found the difference was almost negligible, with the disorder affecting 6% of women and 5.5% of men. (page 14)

⇨ Although Germany is the largest economy in Europe, Internet retail sales in the UK (9.79bn Euros) stood some 80 million Euros ahead of Germany (9.71bn Euros) last year, making the UK Europe's biggest online retail market. (page 15)

⇨ Men are increasingly using the internet for their shopping needs while women still favour high street stores, research reveals. (page 16)

⇨ You do not need a receipt to complain about faulty goods, although it is useful evidence of when and where the purchase was made. (page 17)

⇨ 46% of consumers had bought gifts online in the last year. (page 19)

⇨ The government has announced a major overhaul of consumer rights in the UK with the formation of a new super-body to ensure consumers' interests are better represented. (page 21)

⇨ Consumer credit debt – including problems with credit cards, store cards and charge cards, unsecured personal loans, bank and building society overdrafts. catalogue and mail order debts – remains the biggest problem area related to debt, accounting for 824,000 enquiries to the Citizens' Advice Bureaux. (page 23)

⇨ Britain's personal debt is increasing by £1 million every four minutes. (page 24)

⇨ Average owed by every UK adult is £25,545 (including mortgages). (page 24)

⇨ Trusting UK consumers are not prepared enough for the potential scams that exist online, an ICM survey by Get Safe Online has found, despite the fact that two-thirds (66%) – approximately 19 million people – have been confronted with a suspicious email or website. (page 28)

⇨ Fair trade food and drink sales increased by 52 per cent in 2005. (page 31)

⇨ The value of UK ethical consumerism last year exceeded the sales of 'over-the-counter' beer and cigarettes, according to the Co-operative Bank's annual *Ethical Consumerism Report*. (page 32)

⇨ Consumers consistently say they are concerned about the impact of the products they purchase, and that they prefer to buy from companies that take social and environmental responsibilities seriously. But there remains a major gap between consumers' concern and everyday action. (page 33)

⇨ Two in five consumers (40%) now 'buy free-range products whenever they can' (up from 33% in 2002). (page 34)

⇨ One in four (25%) adults believe it is down to the manufacturers to be more ethical, while a substantial number say it is the government's (28%) or the supermarkets' (24%) responsibility to introduce regulations. (page 35)

⇨ There are 1,500 Fairtrade products available from more than 150 companies, but Fairtrade bananas, for example, still only account for about five per cent of the total British banana market. (page 37)

⇨ Supermarket competitiveness can harm local food economies that sustain our market towns and villages. Their monopoly position in the market allows them to dictate how much they pay farmers, while at the same time seeking out cheaper food from abroad (page 38)

GLOSSARY

Advertising

Advertising is communication between sellers and potential buyers (consumers and other producers). This can be delivered by various media, including radio, television, magazines, newspapers and billboards.

Affluenza

A term coined by psychologist Oliver James, created by combining the two words 'influenza' (an illness) and 'affluence' (wealth). It refers to what James calls a new middle-class mental illness, that of rigorously pursuing consumer goals such as larger houses or new cars. James claims that placing too much importance on material success can lead to mental ill health including depression and anxiety.

Consumer

A consumer is anyone who purchases and uses goods and services.

Consumer durables

A durable item is one which is built to provide service over a period of time, rather than be used up quickly like non-durable items such as food. Consumer durables include items such as home computers, mobile phones and MP3 players. Government figures show that the ownership of consumer durables continued to increase into 2005-2006, with 65% of households owning a home computer, and 79% owning a mobile phone.

Consumer rights

A consumer has the right to expect certain standards in the goods they buy. The law says that the goods must be of satisfactory quality, fit for their purpose and as described. These statutory rights cover all goods bought or hired from a trader, including goods bought in sales.

Credit

A consumer can obtain goods and services before payment, based on an agreement that payment will be made at some point in the future. Other conditions may be imposed. Forms of credit can include personal loans, overdrafts, credit cards, store cards, interest-free credit and hire purchase. However, reliance on credit can result in consumer debt. According to figures from Citizens' Advice, consumer credit debt enquiries have more than doubled in the last eight years.

Ethical consumerism

Buying things that are made ethically – typically, things which do not involve harm to or exploitation of humans, animals or the environment; and also by refusing to buy products or services not made under these principles.

Fair trade

Fair trade is about improving the income that goes to farm workers at the beginning of a supply chain, ensuring that they are paid a fair and stable price for the product supplied. Products produced using fair trade can be identified by the Fairtrade mark.

Scam

A scam is a scheme designed to con consumers out of their money. Scams can take many forms, and are increasingly being perpetrated over the Internet. Some examples include pyramid selling, free gift schemes, lotteries and competitions, investment opportunities, miracle health cures and work-from-home opportunities.

Shopping addiction

Known to psychologists as compulsive buying disorder. A shopping addict is sometimes referred to as a shopaholic. Compulsive or addictive shopping is different from retail therapy; it is a form of behaviour designed to avoid unpleasant reality. It is accompanied by a high which causes the sufferer to lose control and buy many items for which they have no need. A recent study has shown that shopaholics are almost as likely to be men as women, in spite of prior studies suggesting women were more at risk.

INDEX

Additional Resources

Other Issues *titles*

If you are interested in researching further some of the issues raised in *Customers and Consumerism*, you may like to read the following titles in the **Issues** series:

⇨ Vol. 138 *A Genetically Modified Future?* (ISBN 978 1 86168 386 1)
⇨ Vol. 129 *Gambling Trends* (ISBN 978 1 86168 375 5)
⇨ Vol. 110 *Poverty* (ISBN 978 1 86168 343 4)
⇨ Vol. 98 *The Globalisation Issue* (ISBN 978 1 86168 312 0)

For more information about these titles, visit our website at www.independence.co.uk/publicationslist

Useful organisations

You may find the websites of the following organisations useful for further research:

⇨ Advertising Standards Authority: www.asa.org.uk
⇨ Citizens' Advice Bureaux: www.adviceguide.org.uk
⇨ Consumer Credit Counselling Service: www.cccs.co.uk
⇨ Consumer Direct: www.consumerdirect.gov.uk
⇨ Consumer Education: www.consumereducation.org.uk
⇨ Get Safe Online: www.getsafeonline.org
⇨ Mintel: www.mintel.com
⇨ Money Basics: www.moneybasics.co.uk
⇨ National Consumer Council: www.ncc.org.uk

ACKNOWLEDGEMENTS

The publisher is grateful for permission to reproduce the following material.

While every care has been taken to trace and acknowledge copyright, the publisher tenders its apology for any accidental infringement or where copyright has proved untraceable. The publisher would be pleased to come to a suitable arrangement in any such case with the rightful owner.

Chapter One: Consumer Trends

Consumers, © Consumer Education, Consumer spending, © Mintel, Consumer durables, © Crown copyright is reproduced with the permission of Her Majesty's Stationery Officer, Affluenza, © Adfero, Companies branded 'out of touch' by consumers, © National Consumer Council, Advertising, © Consumer Education, Advertising and children, © Advertising Standards Authority, Childhood 'dying in 'spend, spend Britain', © Telegraph Group Ltd, Shopping addiction, © Priory Group, Men are shopaholics too, say psychologists, © Guardian Newspapers Ltd, UK is Europe's number one online retail market, © Mintel, Women and online shopping, © Telegraph Group Ltd.

Chapter Two: Rights and Risks

Consumer rights, © TheSite.org, Your rights, © Crown copyright is reproduced with the permission of Her Majesty's Stationery Office, Changes to consumer rights, © Guardian Newspapers Ltd, Using credit wisely, © Consumer Credit Counselling Service, Rise in problem debt, © Citizens' Advice Bureaux,

Facts and figures, © Credit Action, Debt advice, © Credit Action, Scambuster, © Crown copyright is reproduced with the permission of Her Majesty's Stationery Office, Scammers create web of deceit, © Crown copyright is reproduced with the permission of Her Majesty's Stationery Office.

Chapter Three: Ethical Consumerism

Absolutely ethical, darling!, © Telegraph Group Ltd, Ethical consumerism, © Co-operative bank, What assures consumers? © National Consumer Council, Ethical food, © Mintel, Fair trade, © TheSite.org, The Fairtrade revolution, © Guardian Newspapers Ltd, Supermarkets vs local shops, © TheSite.org.

Illustrations

Pages 1, 14, 23, 32: Don Hatcher; pages 8, 20, 29, 38: Angelo Madrid; pages 11, 16, 27, 31: Simon Kneebone; pages 13, 21: Bev Aisbett.

Photo credits

Page 4: Neil Pickett; pages 5, 13, 15, 18: Independence; page 9: Herbert Berends; page 17: Steve Woods; page 26: Pierre-André Vullioud; page 30: Chris Chidsey; page 33: Marco Michelini; page 35: Meliha Gojak.

And with thanks to the team: Mary Chapman, Sandra Dennis and Jan Haskell.

Lisa Firth
Cambridge
April, 2007